The Spiritual Teacher's Handbook

A Practical Guide to Teaching, Facilitating and
Leadership in a Spiritual Context

The Spiritual Teacher's Handbook

A Practical Guide to Teaching, Facilitating and
Leadership in a Spiritual Context

Dee Apolline

Winchester, UK
Washington, USA

First published by Sixth Books, 2012
Sixth Books is an imprint of John Hunt Publishing Ltd., Laurel House, Station Approach,
Alresford, Hants, SO24 9JH, UK
office1@o-books.net
www.o-books.com

For distributor details and how to order please visit the 'Ordering' section on our website.

Text copyright: Dee Apolline 2010

ISBN: 978 1 84694 662 2

A CIP catalogue record for this book is available from the British Library.

Design: Lee Nash

Printed in the UK by CPI Antony Rowe
Printed in the USA by Offset Paperback Mfrs, Inc

We operate a distinctive and ethical publishing philosophy in all
areas of our business, from our global network of authors to
production and worldwide distribution.

CONTENTS

'"What is a teacher?" I'll tell you: it isn't someone who teaches something, but someone who inspires the student to give of her best in order to discover what she already knows.'

Nabil Alaihi to Athena in *The Witch of Portobello* by Paulo Coelho

Acknowledgements

This book is offered with so much love and gratitude to everyone who has every inspired me to laugh or cry, to stop and stare, to think, feel and evolve.

With extra special thanks to:

The Lovelies, Vaz, Fanoulla, Claudine, Aang, Heather, Sue, Joolz, Lynda, James, Sarah, Cav, Karen and Catrima – without whom this project would not have been created.

My mum – who from Spirit continues to help me learn and understand my world, my life and my experiences with love, humour, and the occasional celestial Slavic back-handed slap …

My amazing friend Vickie, for her constant guidance, support, encouragement, generosity and wisdom – the most humble, loving and real 'guru' I have ever met.

My inspirational friend Caz, who has the most breathtaking commitment to her own evolvement, and who shows me the meaning of true strength, conscious self-awareness and courage.

My dear friend Paul, for helping me to see the true reflection of all of me, and for teaching me how to be in my Truth and strength.

My beautiful son Reuben, who has already taught me how to Let Go and Be more than any formal Spiritual Teacher ever has – and he is only a diddy wee one on the Earth …

October 2010

Introduction

Teaching was never part of the plan. Not my conscious plan, anyway. I am sure that the higher parts of me have always known I would be here doing what I am doing. But all of it feels like it happened by accident.

As I look back upon the many varied and often seemingly unconnected events my life, I see that every single one of them has worked together to get me to this point, like each individual musician in an orchestra ... each part playing its own tune, but together with others, creating a beautiful symphony. Every one of those events has led me here, to this point, to the creation of this book.

I have been blessed to experience a wide range of learning opportunities, teaching styles and skills as part of my own spiritual journey. Those have partly led to this guidance.

I am struck by how many teachers seek to empower their students to find their own Truth – and how many still believe that there are strict 'rules' that must be followed in order for students to connect with their spirituality. It feels to me that we are entering a newer time of celebrating our humanness as people and as teachers – making spirituality more accessible – whilst recognising that none of us knows it all, or indeed can tell others what their truth is.

I have come to several conclusions that, for me, underpin all of the work that I now do based on what I have learned along the way.

Firstly, I may be a Spiritual Teacher, but I am still very much a student on my journey – and often my 'students' are my greatest 'teachers'.

Secondly, I don't know the answers. I only know *my* answers; the ones my life has taught me; the ones I have been willing to learn from. I don't believe that any teacher has 'the answers' for anyone else. I do believe that all we can do as teachers is to hold a space for others to find their own answers; their own Truth in whatever ways feel right for them. In fact, my Truth changes as my learning and understanding develops.

Thirdly, I am not an expert or indeed a guru. I don't consider myself to be a Master, even though when wearing one of my 'hats' as an Angelic Reiki Teacher, that is how I am recognised by title. I don't believe that any of us are 'Masters' of anything other than ourselves. I am an ordinary person who is able to share what I have learnt as a teacher and as a continuing student, and it feels like an honour to do so.

Fourthly, I am still learning about my journey and who I am. I am not 'Buddha Enlightened'. As a spiritual being having a human experience, I still have meltdowns, I get angry with The Universe when I Don't Understand, I love watching *South Park*, and comedy swearing makes me giggle. I am, however, also committed to learning more about my own journey, including accepting ALL of me so I can come to a place of peace and unconditional love as quickly and easily as possible (and hopefully with some humour thrown in along the way!).

I am fascinated by learning. One of the aspects of how we learn that intrigues me the most is how we do so energetically. Carl Jung described the 'the collective unconscious' – the part of the unconscious mind shared by humankind – almost 100 years ago.

This corresponds with what we are now coming to learn from the field of Quantum physics.

Quantum physicists have been able to demonstrate that we are all connected. This has been proven through experiments showing that a change in the behaviour of one photon (light particle) can lead to a change in the behaviour of another photon which is separated by a massive distance. This theory, 'entanglement theory', could explain why Spiritual Teachers who bring through new knowledge sometimes find that another teacher, whom they have never met and who lives in another part of the world, has brought through the same new knowledge.

This has led me to question whether any of us who are teachers are ever bringing through something 'new' or 'groundbreaking'. I have come across the exact same theories being presented by completely different teachers, even though they think that their message is unique. I guess that they have been tuned into that same wonderful amazing collective consciousness at the same time as other people. So I feel that all learning opportunities are actually recycled. They are, however, all still needed, as each can be a gateway for a student to learn more about what they need to know, at different places on the planet.

The contents of this book are based on *my learning* from my teachers – some of whom I have had the privilege to meet, some of whom I haven't, all of whom have contributed to what I share with you in this book. None of this knowledge is 'new'; it is – like all learning opportunities – recycled. However, it is presented in a new way, hopefully in ways that help you to reach your greatest potential as a Spiritual Teacher.

I have realised that as I continue to learn and grow, many of my experiences, beliefs, attitudes and values as a Spiritual Teacher are being challenged. I hope that by sharing these, I can help you to feel empowered to your Truth as a teacher of others – and most importantly a teacher of yourself. I really don't know the answers, but I hope that we can together develop a community that supports one another's evolvement for the benefit of all.

I feel blessed to have been able to bring together my love of facilitating learning opportunities with all my experiences on my spiritual journey to create this.

What Do We Mean by 'Spiritual Teaching'?

There are many terms that refer to the process of empowering others to learn, develop and grow – which we will explore in this chapter. As well as there being many terms for the process, there are also several definitions for each term. On this basis, I have given suggested summaries for each one below.

Teaching – The process of supporting others to learn, often through instruction. Usually, the learning focuses on knowledge-based information.

Training – The process of supporting a person's development, leading to improved performance in a specific area. The focus is usually on the development of knowledge, skills, and attitudes.

Facilitation – The process of holding a space for others to develop and learn at their own pace. Facilitators recognise that the learner already knows the answers, and is trying to remember them.

Education – Activities that aim to develop knowledge, skills, moral values and understanding in all areas of life.

Preaching – Making statements with a view to asking others to accept or comply with a particular view, belief or way of life.

Leadership – Giving guidance and direction to others.

Coaching – Empowering an individual to reflect upon and own their situation so that they can then decide upon the direction they would like to take to achieve success in a certain area. Involves identifying the actions necessary for that success to be achieved.

Mentoring – Advising, supporting, guiding another – allowing a person to try activities and encouraging them to reflect upon their learning.

Tutoring – One-to-one teaching or development.

Learning – A process that allows us to adapt to change through the acquiring of knowledge, skills and attitudes. It can be used to get individuals to conform, but can be used to encourage us to think for ourselves.

Is it important that we label what we do?

How we communicate what we do is very important for us as well as our students. We use language as the means by which we do this. Using language, we convey what the aims for our learning opportunities are, and what our role is. So on this basis, it could be said that the language we use is very important. I would suggest, however, that we are often limited by language as a means of *accurately* communicating exactly what we are doing.

Each of us interprets words, labels – and the concepts that they convey – based on our own individual experiences and perceptions. Some people, for example, see the word 'teaching' and associate it with school-based rote learning or with that sense of separation where 'teachers' are said to have all of the knowledge, and their role is to 'impart' that knowledge onto their students. Other people might perceive the term 'teaching' as a general word linked to a learning opportunity.

I would suggest that it is more helpful to convey the intentions behind the learning opportunity – this is how people can get more of an idea of your approach. For example, is your intention to communicate knowledge you feel an audience does not have, or could your intention be to empower or enable them to develop their confidence or understanding in a particular area?

This point can be clearly illustrated when we consider which of the activities listed on the previous page empower the development of passions and potential within people. Depending on the intentions of the teacher, every single activity listed can be empowering – including preaching – if the teacher intends for it to be empowering! To that end, every single one of the listed activities can be disempowering, if the teacher seeks to make themselves more powerful than their students. It all depends on the intentions of the teacher. We will explore communication in more detail in the chapter on Teaching Skills, but for now, it seems, that some clarity around how I use language in this book may help.

What I would suggest – for the purposes of this book at least – is that 'teaching' is a word that could easily summarise most activities that lead to learning. In fact, we may use any combination of these activities when we are in a 'teaching' role, including facilitating or coaching. In choosing to refer to all of these activities under the general title of 'teaching', I am just using language in a very simplistic way to try to convey a range of ways of supporting the development of others and providing opportunities for others to learn.

I have also chosen to use the word 'student' to describe people taking part in these learning opportunities; however, I do so loosely. We could use other terms such as learner, delegate or participant. I feel that we are all each of these, so again I feel that the choice of word is a question of semantics. I would ask that – again for the purposes of this book – it is always remembered that, in every learning opportunity, we are all students and teachers (or participants and facilitators) together.

Attitudes, intentions, skills and knowledge
Some students believe that the knowledge or experience of a Spiritual Teacher is more important than the teacher's attitudes

– often because our education system values and rewards knowledge.

Also, some students value a teacher having a lot of knowledge because of how they prefer to learn. If, for example, a student's preferred learning style is that of a 'theorist', they are likely to prefer learning theories and knowledge before considering how to apply them. This will be explored in more detail in the chapter on Accelerated Learning.

However, the skills and attitudes of a teacher could be said to be as important as the knowledge that a teacher has (if not more important), within a spiritual context.

A teacher may have considerable knowledge and experience, but if they find it difficult to use teaching skills effectively to support their students being able to make use of that knowledge for themselves, or to have their own empowering experiences, then that knowledge and experience may not be as accessible to the students. A teacher may have considerable knowledge and experience in a particular area, and may have the attitude that they are an 'expert' or that students will never have as much knowledge/skills/experience as them. This can reinforce the self-doubts of students. This can make it more difficult for students to learn, because they are less able to see themselves as being able to develop as much as their teacher has. Students often have some feelings of doubt and uncertainty about whether or not they are capable of learning; so it is vital to empower students to believe that they are capable learners – this will help them to have confidence in themselves.

An attitude of empowerment, love and support can help to create a more powerful learning environment than using knowledge alone. Without this attitude, students might not feel as safe to explore what they can do in the learning opportunity, which makes it more difficult for them to learn and be empowered. This will also be described in more detail in the chapter on Accelerated Learning.

When teaching spiritual subjects, is it important that our students come to believe the same things that we do? Do their attitudes need to match ours?

This could be said to be 'preaching' – which some people might feel is inappropriate. I would suggest, however, that it again depends of the intentions of the teacher, and on the context.

It may be, for example, that there are certain principles that matter to you, e.g. attitudes around respecting each other, or about energetic cleansing or about protection. You may well wish others to develop the same attitudes as you in some areas. This may be entirely helpful to others. It is important, however, to be conscious of how much of this is ego-based, and how much is about supporting the development of students in an empowering way.

It is important to consider the role that our egos play as teachers. It can feel good when our students come to believe the same things as us: it can reinforce our own beliefs and values, and can help us to feel validated. This is a particular issue in a spiritual context, where much of what gets taught is considered to be 'less acceptable' to mainstream society, or 'less valid' or 'unscientific' or 'unproven'. Often, as Spiritual Teachers, we will have had to overcome the many doubts of other people, from close friends and families through to strangers, and this can mean that we feel a need for that validation even more. We will explore this in more detail throughout this book.

However, truly empowered learners are encouraged to find their own attitudes and beliefs, which may be completely different from our own. Some people would suggest that all students know everything that they need to know already. If so, our roles as 'teachers' may simply be to help them to remember what they know, and enable them to connect with what they are passionate about.

Self-development questions
1. What is it about your message(s) that is so important to your students?
2. How would you feel if your students developed different beliefs or attitudes from you in the areas that you consider to be fundamentally important to you?
3. How would you then respond to your students if that happened?
4. If it would it be challenging for you to remain in a supportive, loving and accepting space, do you know what would cause you to find it difficult (e.g. being reminded of a situation where your views may not have been accepted from another time in your life)? Is this something that you could look to heal?
5. What would help you to remain in a supportive, loving and accepting space with all of your students?

Is spiritual teaching an important time for us to share our own personal journeys with our students?

It is helpful to share some aspects of our personal journeys, so that students feel more comfortable and confident that we have had some experiences that have led us to this teaching role.

There are two types of personal experiences that can safely be shared:

a) experiences of magic and wonder in your spiritual journey (for example, seeing crystals falling out of the sky, feathers appearing at key stages on your journey)

Sharing your own experiences of magic and wonder in your spiritual journey can support students in being able to consider how anything may be possible, and to encourage them to connect with what they may experience in their own lives. Also it can give students ideas of which new directions might interest them as well. When describing these experiences, it is worth bearing in mind that sometimes students can then feel that they won't ever reach the stage where those kind of experiences could happen to them, so it helps to be in a place of humility – of recognising that special experiences happen to all of us. Also, be mindful that your ego (and your students' egos) can have fun here – it can be easy to step into a space of 'Listen to what happened to me!'

b) personal stories of challenges that do not cause you emotional upset while you are sharing the experiences. This includes difficulties in relationships, addictions, childhood trauma.

As for personal experiences, it is usually not necessary to go into detail on many aspects of our own life story – especially in describing traumatic life stories such as abuse. If you are experiencing an emotional reaction to the stories that you are sharing, you may trigger an emotional response in your students, where some of them may feel that they want to – or should – emotionally support you in that moment. At this point in time, you are no longer holding the space as a teacher, leader, or facilitator because you are in need. It could be said, however, that – in this moment – you truly are an equal with your students.

If you are still processing or healing an aspect of your life (in other words, if you still feel emotion on any level when thinking about it or talking about it), you may not be ready to share that aspect with students – it is important that you leave your needs for support outside of the learning environment.

The key is to check with yourself whether what you would like to share is *completely relevant* to what you are supporting your students to learn about. Students can find it difficult to engage with any workshop that is a 'Me Workshop' – in other words, workshops where the teacher just talks about their experiences. These kinds of workshops are often disempowering because they take time away from the students and their ability to have their own precious learning experiences.

By being conscious of your intentions for the development of the group, you may find that your intuition guides you to know what to share and what not to share, and to what extent; however, you need to be as balanced and self-aware as possible to ensure that it is your intuition, and not your ego, guiding you.

As with all guiding principles, there are sometimes exceptions – which require a significant amount of conscious self-awareness on the part of the teacher. Here is an example from one of my own teaching experiences.

I was facilitating a three-day Angelic Reiki Teacher course. Throughout the first day, I kept hearing the angels saying 'Share your current life challenges in this group' and 'This a safe space for you to heal.' I spent the whole day debating this – actually, arguing – with the angels, explaining that it would compromise my position as someone holding the space for others ... and I had already written a book and a course which focuses on not using teaching opportunities as spaces for your own healing!

At the end of the first day, one of the students said 'I have a message from the angels for you, Dee. They're saying that you need to allow yourself to let go and receive healing in this space.' I explained why I didn't feel this was appropriate. Another student piped up and said 'I've been getting the same message too.' I questioned the appropriateness of this for some time before I eventually let go. For the following two days, I realised I was – probably for the first time – truly not separated from and equal to my students in their eyes, and we collectively and equally experienced some of the most transformative healing I have ever come across. We all held the space for each other equally to process some of our greatest challenges.

In this space, it was completely appropriate to the needs of this particular group to do so. I then tried a similar approach in a different group, but found it to be inappropriate to the needs of that group.

What this taught me was the value of continuing to choose to hold the space for others and not share the emotional challenges that I have not yet resolved. As with all principles, very occasionally something else is needed. In the Angelic Reiki course, I questioned my guidance and those of others many times to ensure that it truly was the most appropriate thing to do in those circumstances. I let go whilst being very conscious and present about what I was doing and why.

We will explore more about this in the next chapter.

What are the benefits of providing learning opportunities for others, as opposed to them reading a book on a subject?

- Provides students with the opportunity to have more personal experiences and to develop their skills
- Can help students to develop more confidence in their knowledge or abilities
- Can help students to understand some of their experiences
- Can assist in the process of change and growth of individuals, groups and the wider collective
- Gives students the opportunity to meet new people as part of their spiritual journey
- Helps students find support for their own journey and learning
- Enables students to make connections with other souls who they may have links to energetically
- Can enhance the process of remembering
- Can raise collective energies through the energetic power of groups coming together; this can raise individual energies too, which can lead to more powerful experiences

– and benefit individuals, groups and the planet
- Can help to empower people to recognise the abilities, skills and knowledge they have and are capable of further developing

Having considered what spiritual teaching involves, we will explore the role of a Spiritual Teacher in more detail.

The Role of a Spiritual Teacher

There are many aspects to being a Spiritual Teacher – practical, emotional, psychological, administrative, and energetic. We might prefer some of these aspects more than others – it is quite common, for example, for Spiritual Teachers to prefer the 'teaching' part rather than the practical administrative stuff like completing tax returns! In this chapter, we will explore some of these aspects in more detail.

The role of a teacher

During a course, workshop or class, you will, as a Spiritual Teacher, be responsible for a range of activities. You can:

- Introduce the session
- Identify guiding principles with the group / set clear boundaries / discuss expectations that you all have of each other
- Explain the aim of exercises
- Inform learners of timings – and keep to them
- Clear the space, self and group energetically
- Maintain the physical, emotional and energetic safety and wellbeing of yourself and others
- Ground yourself and others
- Lead discussions
- Hold the space
- Respond to the needs of the group
- Communicate accessibly (not too much jargon!)
- Be clear about the content of the course
- Inspire students to find out what they can do for themselves
- Motivate students to try new skills and seek their Truth
- Check the understanding of students
- Encourage students to question and explore

- Give students choices about what they learn, experience and how to apply this in their everyday lives
- Be in a place of humility
- Be conscious of own sense of balance and need for healing – looking after yourself as well as your students
- Be supportive of the learning and experiences of students, no matter where they are at on their journeys
- Empower students to make changes if they would like to
- Manage challenges that arise from a place of self-awareness, love and compassion
- Summarise and reflect upon key points with students

Outside a workshop or class, you can:

- Make a commitment to look after your own needs for physical, mental, emotional and spiritual wellbeing and growth
- Continue to learn and evolve your knowledge, understanding and skills
- Prepare course content
- Book a suitable venue
- Advertise your courses
- Prepare course information packs, workbooks, handouts
- Take bookings and answer queries
- Establish if any students have any individual needs during the course, e.g. if reasonable adjustments are needed by disabled students, or if a student has any dietary requirements
- Communicate what learners need to know about the course
- Create a loving, comfortable, inspiring, healing and safe environment
- Familiarise yourself with where the toilets / fire exits of the venue are
- Check that equipment is working before the course begins

- Self-evaluate your skills, knowledge, attitudes and approach after the workshop or class
- Evaluate course content, quality of resources, and the comfort of the venue
- Connect students to each other so that they can continue to support each other
- Carry out personal administration – arrange insurance, maintain membership of professional bodies, manage finances and prepare tax returns.

Self-development questions
1. What have been your most challenging experiences as a student in spiritual and non-spiritual workshops and classes? What made them challenging for you?
2. What have been your most inspirational experiences as a student in spiritual and non-spiritual workshops and classes? What made them inspirational for you?

What skills and qualities could an 'Inspirational Spiritual Teacher' have?

These will vary from individual to individual – we are all different and indeed unique, and bring our own personalities to our workshops. The following is a list of general skills and qualities that support the empowerment of students:

- Effective communication and presentation skills
- Understanding and honouring confidentiality
- Patience
- Ability to treat all students equally whilst respecting individual differences and needs
- Integrity
- Organisational skills

- Effective time management
- Motivating and empowering others
- Encouraging others
- Friendliness
- Approachability
- Active listening skills
- Being an effective facilitator
- Flexibility
- Humility
- Commitment to your own growth and development
- A non-judgemental attitude
- Openness to many different viewpoints
- Balance
- Ability to 'hold the space' for others to learn and develop
- Ability to clear space, self and group energetically
- Self-awareness/consciousness of your own state of balance and need for healing
- Ability to change the pace and content of a workshop as needed to respond the needs of the group
- Being an effective channel
- The intention to be in a place of unconditional love, Truth and compassion – knowing how to return to this space if needed
- Openness to questions / being challenged on your own perspectives and beliefs

The following methods can support you in your journey to becoming an Inspirational Spiritual Teacher:

- Practising what you plan to deliver
- Conscious self-awareness
- Self-evaluation – especially from a place of humility
- Training/learning about being a Spiritual Teacher
- Underlying knowledge

- Having a passion for teaching
- Ability to use effective communication skills

Self-development questions
1. What do you think your main sources of satisfaction are/will be as an Inspirational Spiritual Teacher?
2. What do you feel will be / are your greatest challenges as an inspirational teacher?
3. What will help you to overcome any challenges so that you can be the Inspirational Spiritual Teacher that you choose to be?
4. What skills and qualities do you have?
5. Which skills and qualities would you like to develop more?
6. How can you develop these further?

The 'Inspirational Spiritual Teacher'

Every teacher has their own style of teaching, based on their experiences, their background, their soul and their personality. These are suggested attributes and principles in spiritual teaching that can help to inspire and empower students to get the most out of learning opportunities and stand in their own strength and Truth as quickly and powerfully as possible.

1. Humility
An Inspirational Spiritual Teacher is able to publicly recognise that they are still learning too, even when they are in a teaching, facilitating or leadership role. Your learners are partners in the learning journey, not your subordinates. Being open to challenge, and understanding that your Truths may not be other people's Truths, is an important part of this.

Invite your learners to check what resonates with them so that learners are empowered to feel more confident about recognising what they already do know as their own Truth. Respond to questions and challenges with love and acceptance – be conscious of your ego's needs to 'be right' to help you remain in a place of respectful love as much as possible.

2. Facilitation

An Inspirational Spiritual Teacher takes on a facilitative role as much as possible so that learners have the space to explore their own ideas and abilities. An Inspirational Spiritual Teacher will not judge what is contributed.

3. Ability to leave personal issues outside the learning environment

An Inspirational Spiritual Teacher is able to act as a model for others, 'holding the space' for others to develop. Any personal agendas, personal prejudices and personal problems need to be left outside of the learning environment. Do share personal experiences that it is relevant for you to share; however, if you still have an emotional reaction in any way about your experiences (even if you think you can contain it), learners will feel this. This is likely to be perceived by your learners as you being in need of support, and they may want to give it to you. If this happens, this is likely to take the learners out of their role as learners, and alters the dynamic of the learning situation. It is not their responsibility to support you. You may, however, be guided on occasion that it is relevant to share some issues. If so, do be conscious of your sharing and what it might mean for your group.

4. Commitment to your own self-awareness and development

An Inspirational Spiritual Teacher recognises that we are all continuing to grow and learn about ourselves and our journeys and are 'works in progress' – including the teacher. A commitment to learning and healing as much as possible reflects self-awareness of your own journey. This includes regular spiritual practice and knowing what your professional limitations are – including knowing when to refer your students to other sources of guidance.

5. Spiritual hygiene

An Inspirational Spiritual Teacher is aware of maintaining a balanced energetic space before, during and after workshops, and is committed to clearing space energetically in order to maintain a safe space.

6. Equality of opportunity

An Inspirational Spiritual Teacher ensures that everyone in the learning group has an equal opportunity to develop their skills, ideas, knowledge and attitudes. This includes avoiding the use of jargon which can exclude some learners if they don't know what you mean. Even terms such as 'grounding' which are commonly used in a spiritual context may not be understood by all learners, so ensure that you make all of your learning opportunities accessible to all by not making assumptions about what others know.

7. Confidentiality

An Inspirational Spiritual Teacher respects the right of every learner to feel, say and think whatever they want to without talking about 'who said what' outside of the learning environment.

8. Acting as a model

An Inspirational Spiritual Teacher reflects the behaviour, attitudes and skills contained in the workshop (for example, being in a place of unconditional love when facilitating a workshop on unconditional love or having worked through issues around money or weight if facilitating workshops in these areas).

9. Sense of humour

By being relaxed ourselves about our own journeys, we can allow others to be more relaxed about theirs. The challenges we all face at times are made so much easier through humour!

10. Knowing there is no such thing as 'perfect'!

Or maybe there is – accepting yourself as you are, whilst being conscious of your own journey and developmental needs.

Key Spiritual Concepts

Teaching in a spiritual context can involve dealing with a wide range of definitions, beliefs, approaches and expectations. There are as many theories as there are people, and so trying to develop our understanding of core principles can be a challenge. It is not like teaching people basic arithmetic where the clear rules state that 1 + 1 = 2! Often you are working with such a wide range of possible belief systems and experiences, that all that can be consistently achieved is ensuring that students check what resonates with them!

Core definitions

This is not an exhaustive list of definitions or concepts that are found in a spiritual context. They are, however, some key terms that I hope are useful. These definitions are my own suggested definitions, based on researching many others, and relating these to my own experiences. You may have your own preferred definitions – please refer to whatever resonates most with you.

Spirituality – An exploration of something 'greater' than our human selves (spirit); a multidimensional reality beyond our physical selves, and beyond our material (earthly) experiences. It is a personal experience but one that can connect us to something greater than ourselves. Religions are an expression of spirituality, but someone can be spiritual without being religious.

Grounding – Connecting to being in the present moment, and to your current physical, mental, emotional and spiritual reality.

Chakras – From a Sanskrit word that means 'wheel turning'. They are considered to be vortices or balls of energy – energy centres – that act as gateways for the flow of energy through the energy body and physical body. There were originally considered to be 7 major chakras, but some now say that there are 12, others 36, and yet other teachers would say that there are hundreds or even thousands.

Ego – This is the part of us that connects with the conscious mind. It defines us as an individual by connecting with our personality. It is the prism through which we perceive ourselves. It helps us to live our material life and supports our physical survival. It connects with our free will.

Higher Self – A 'Divine blueprint' containing all of the information about who we are, the purpose(s) of this life, the story of every other lifetime and our highest potential. It is said to know what is for our 'Highest Good' – in other words, what will help our souls to evolve. It communicates to us through our intuition, gut feelings and sudden changes in our lives.

Aura – High-frequency layers of energy that surround the physical body. Each layer has a different function – for example, the etheric layer, the emotional body, the mental body and so on. Auras can be photographed using Kirlian photography.

Soul – The spiritual or Divine part of human existence. If the soul is described as being like the body, and the spirit as an overcoat over the body, then the spirit could be said to be the part of ourselves that contains our personality and ego. Our spirit is only needed to help us with our journey in this lifetime. One soul could have a different spirit for every lifetime. Mediums connect with spirit, i.e. with the personality we would have connected with in this lifetime.

Intuition – Literally 'in-tuition'; connecting with one's own internal guidance / Spiritual Teacher, or one's own Truth from the heart. The word 'intuition' is said to come from the Latin word *intueri*, which is often roughly translated as meaning 'to look inside' or 'to contemplate'. We can use our senses to help us to interpret our in-tuition; sight (clairvoyance), sound (clairaudience), thought (claircognisance), feeling (clairsentience) and smell.

Ego versus Higher Self

Two of the more significant concepts that are often referred to in a spiritual teaching context are those of the ego and the Higher Self. In my experience, there is often a lot of presumption around what these terms mean, and often a lot of judgement also. It is often perceived that 'ego is bad' and 'Higher Self is good'; however, each serves a purpose – and presents its own challenges also. It feels important to highlight these here.

The following exploration of the ego and Higher Self is based on the work of James Harvey Stout (deceased).

How our ego helps us:

- Helps us to define our personalities and individual identity/style
- Provides a sense of stability; however, it is constantly changing, which can make it unstable/ungrounded
- Can help us to develop our self-esteem and assertiveness so that we can stand in our own power
- Tries to make sense of the world around us, and then analyses what it perceives – which we use in decision making

- Helps us to function – by getting us out of bed in the morning, getting dressed and to work etc
- Helps us to make choices in all aspects of our lives – choosing jobs, education, lifestyle
- Seeks to protect us from doing something it perceives as embarrassing or unhelpful to us
- Can ensure that behaviour is consistent with identity/values
- Can make life easier in the short term – tries to stop us having to take responsibility for our actions
- Helps us to focus on our memories
- Helps us to define personal boundaries – including when raising children
- Once we know who we are, our ego allows us to let go of who we are – so a strong and clearly defined ego is an important part of our development spiritually
- Provides us with many lessons
- Provides a source of entertainment at times

Challenges of having an ego:

- Separates us from others through its focus on individuality – particularly because it focuses on its own interests
- Can make it difficult for us to honestly reflect upon ourselves – can contribute to our 'blind spots'
- If the ego is unrecognised or not respected, it can seek out respect from others
- Intervenes to prevent connecting with our intuition and Higher Self
- Can prevent us from believing in ourselves and so fulfilling our potential
- Can make it difficult for us to build effective relationships with others
- Can be competitive

- Can control us if we allow this, which can lead to an inflated sense of self-importance, seeking status – it can be 'all about me!'
- Sometimes our will and ego can lead us to try to create or achieve that which we *perceive* to be for our best, which can then be problematic

How our Higher Self helps us:

- Helps us to connect with our life purpose
- Helps us to remember lessons from other lifetimes so that we can grow and develop
- Can present opportunities for our growth and development
- Can help us make decisions about our lives that support our growth and progress
- Communicates with our soul/Source
- Is always there – even though we may not always be consciously aware of this
- Protects us and keeps us safe (through 'gut feelings')
- Can help us to progress in our life / soul journey more quickly
- Helps us to connect with Love and Wisdom
- Helps us to feel peaceful and centred
- Can aid creativity
- Helps us to connect with forgiveness, unconditional love and compassion
- Supports us to act in 'our Truth'
- Values and understands the challenges that are presented to us
- Could be said to be 'always right'

Challenges of having a Higher Self:

- It can be a challenge in the short term when our Higher Self communicates with us using a sudden life change – the changes can be disruptive
- Is not logical
- Often requires surrendering the will, which can cause internal conflict and dissonance
- Can lead to significant changes in relationships and other aspects of our lives which we may not have been consciously expecting – this can lead to experiencing difficult emotions if we do not feel we understand the purpose of what has happened
- We usually cannot consciously remember much of what our Higher Self knows, and so can find it hard to understand the 'bigger picture'
- It is always there, and so even when we try to avoid undertaking a lesson consciously, the lessons can present in other ways – in other words, it can't be ignored!
- Could be said to be 'always right'

Why do we need to be aware of this as Spiritual Teachers?
It is very important to ensure that you don't judge students, or treat them differently if they are in their ego – indeed you will sometimes or often be working from your own! As Jack Engler, Harvard psychologist and Buddhist teacher, said: 'You have to be somebody before you can be nobody.'

We can feel – as teachers – that it is 'not a good thing' to be in our ego, or that someone who is needs to change that.

All of us, when we are in our ego, are still engaged in our own journey and our own path of growth and development. By negating the ego (which is a common response in spiritual contexts), we are preventing ourselves from integrating, respecting and recognising all aspects of ourselves. I believe that integrating all aspects of ourselves is what we need to do in order to reach enlightenment.

You, as a teacher, however much experience you have, are likely at times to connect with your ego. I would suggest that a loving approach would be to remain conscious and acknowledge this to yourself. You can then choose what happens with where you are at, and make changes if you feel that is needed.

One last observation on the ego ...

I think the ego is a tricky thing to suppress as a parent! Since becoming a mother, I have realised that no matter how I choose to work with my ego, it will be present and proud every time anyone says anything complimentary about my child: all my ego wants to do is shout 'Yes! Yes! Yes! You are SO right ...' So my latest lesson (thanks to my son) is that The Ego Has A Purpose So It Must Stay ;)

Accelerated Learning

In this chapter and the next, we will think about how we, as individuals, learn – psychologically and energetically. Every individual has their own preferred style(s) of learning – we will identify our own preferred styles and apply this to see how other people have different learning styles. By understanding the ways that people learn, we – as teachers – can help our students to learn more effectively and remember their learning.

There are many factors which affect how people learn as adults:

- Their motivations to learn
- How grounded and protected they are or perceive themselves to be
- Their interest in the subject area
- Linking their learning to past, present or future experiences
- Practising what they have been taught
- Learning in an informal, stimulating and comfortable environment
- Receiving clear answers to questions that they have about their own spiritual journey in ways that they feel positive about
- Time to learn and reflect
- Willingness to be present in the learning opportunity
- Being inspired by observing others' learning experiences
- Getting in our own way – letting our mind affect our feelings of safety / ability in front of others
- Attitudes/confidence
- Influences of others as well as self
- Nervousness/shyness/fear of 'the unknown'
- Being 'put on the spot' by a teacher
- Scepticism

- Methods of teaching delivery

What motivates people to attend spiritual workshops?
There are many reasons – here are some suggestions:

- Wanting/needing a greater understanding about their journeys/lives/relationships
- Feeling unfulfilled in their lives
- Wanting to feel happier
- Desiring personal growth
- Needing change
- Needing to resolve problems in relationships
- Seeking material or work success
- Wanting to feel more balanced / more at peace with themselves
- Meeting other spiritual/like-minded people where it's easier to be themselves
- They were guided by intuition or dreams
- To help understand a sad experience, e.g. losing a loved one
- To learn new skills or evolve existing ones, e.g. connecting with those in Spirit – including loved ones who have passed into spirit
- Friends/colleagues have done the same
- They were encouraged to by someone else, e.g. partner, tutor, friend
- Wanting to challenge themselves
- There may be contracts (energetic and other) between one student and another, or indeed between a student and you, as the teacher, that need to be fulfilled

As teachers, we need to understand why people are attending our courses. This will affect their motivation to learn; for example, if a student is encouraged to attend a workshop on inner child work, but is only doing it to keep their partner happy, how will that affect their learning and experiences?

We will identify our own preferred styles of learning, but first we will consider the psychological theory behind learning, and then link this to energetic learning as we move through different models.

The Competency Staircase

According to psychology-based principles, for any of us to become competent at doing something, we need to learn about it, and practise it. The more we learn and practise, the easier it becomes – our brain (or our heart!) recognises that this is something that we have done before. So the brain (or heart) remembers how to do it, so that we can perform a task more easily than the last time we did it.

For example, for those of us who can swim, we don't have to think about how we float or move in the water whilst we breathe; we just move through the water. Our brains recognise this action as one we have done many times before and we are therefore able to swim unconsciously.

There is a theory known as the 'Competency Staircase' which describes how we learn to do a task over time, and become more and more competent, the more we practise. The Competency Staircase is divided into four stages. We will now look at this theory in a little more detail.

This model has been beautifully illustrated using the analogy of learning to drive. It was developed by Jonathan Emmins and the training team at the National Union of Students.

Stage One: Unconscious incompetence
- This is the stage at which we usually start. We are unconsciously incompetent – we are unaware of what it is we don't know.

- We may have sat in the passenger seat and navigated for others, so driving looks easy. We are at this stage unaware of what it is we don't know, the range of skills involved in driving a car.

Stage Two: Conscious incompetence

- We suddenly realise what we have to learn. We know what it is that we DON'T know! This can be a frustrating time for some people; they may quit at this point, if they are not motivated to carry on.
- That first driving lesson is a real eye-opener – we sit behind the wheel of a car and suddenly realise how much we have to learn; how complex driving is.

Stage Three: Conscious competence

- We know how to do it right, but we need to think hard to keep it going. This stage involves small progressive steps, during which our feelings of awkwardness gradually give way to a sense of achievement as we become more skilled.
- We've been kangaroo-hopping as we drive down the road and suddenly we are beginning to put things together. With practice and experience we are beginning to acquire knowledge and skills.

Stage Four: Unconscious competence

- We can do it – we don't even think about it. The process seems natural and easy and does not require so much concentration.
- For us to be able to apply a skill unconsciously – without thinking about it – we have to have repeated that action 200 times, according to this theory. This gives you an idea of how important practising skills is!

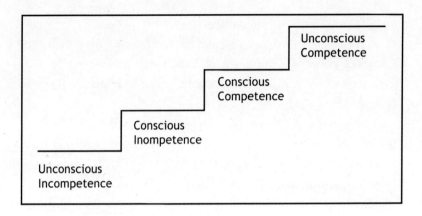

Most people who come to courses and workshops are probably at the 'conscious incompetence' stage – they know they need to develop, and want help to do that. We can help them by giving them opportunities to develop the knowledge that they need and time to practice using the relevant skills. It is then up to them to go away and keep practising until they are competent, either on their own, with friends or more formally in further development groups and workshops. This is also the stage when people learn the most.

Generally speaking, it is said that to move up the Competency Staircase, from one stage to the next, individuals have to fully experience each stage. That is, they have to practise at that stage over and over again until they feel comfortable with it, before they can move on. In effect, you test out your new skills to make sure that you are doing things right, and can do them again.

What about 'flukes'?
There are exceptions to this process of fully experiencing each stage of the competency staircase – for example, with the occurrence of 'flukes'; when individuals perform competently with little or no experience of the skill. A classic example of this is when people play pool or snooker, and despite not being consciously great players, they seem to play unusually well (this

usually involves some alcohol!).

In these situations, because we are not focused on performing using our conscious mind, the ego can't step in – we can leap up to 'unconscious competence' without going through the learning cycle 200 times per step.

The mind/ego gets in the way when we then try to focus on performing; it says 'you can't do it', and then our learning focus becomes psychological rather than intuitive. This is when we go back to learning using this model.

Maybe alcohol in these circumstances helps to drown out the ego/mind?

We can also have strong spiritual experiences that begin anywhere on the Competency Staircase, including 'fluke-like' experiences that are at the unconscious competence stage.

For example, it is possible to have a powerful channelling experience, having never consciously learned to channel. Once someone has a powerful unconscious experience, they may then focus on learning consciously about what has happened uncon-sciously – they are then aware of what they 'don't know, but need to or would like to know', and then are more likely to go through the process of climbing the Competency Staircase.

The Competency Staircase, the ego, Higher Self and intuition

It could be said that the journey of moving up the competency staircase is also a journey of moving from working with the ego to working with the Higher Self in a way that is comfortable for the learner.

This model supports the attempts by the ego to say 'you can't do it' or 'it will take you ages to learn how to do that'. It keeps the learner focused on the individual task rather than the bigger picture. It is in fact one of the ways we have been conditioned to learn.

One of my experiences has been how much more quickly

students seem to learn and develop when in a spiritual teaching context, compared with more traditional skills development training opportunities. This may be for many reasons. It may be that students are more comfortable exploring personal development. Perhaps they are more interested and motivated by the need to understand themselves as opposed to understanding a process, which is what training opportunities can focus on. It may also be that students in a spiritual context are learning to remember something that they already 'know' and so are already competent, but just need to develop their confidence. Whatever the reasons, one of the real privileges of being a Spiritual Teacher is to be present during the rapid development of an individual or group.

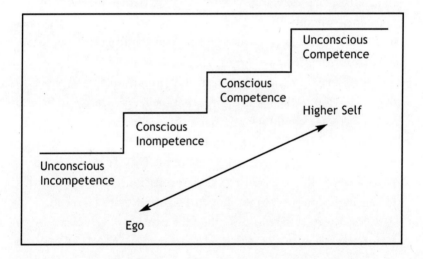

We will now consider how we can further improve the learning outcomes for our students psychologically and energetically. We will begin with Accelerated Learning.

The MASTER model of Accelerated Learning
(Colin Rose, 1985)

Learning involves the development of existing knowledge, skills and attitudes – and the acquisition of new knowledge, skills and attitudes.

A new method of enhancing learning began its development in the 1970s. Accelerated Learning, as it was named, is more than one theory – it is a collection of studies by psychological researchers who estimate that its techniques can achieve at least a 300% improvement in how quickly people learn, and how well they remember what they have learnt.

Accelerated Learning stimulates the conscious and unconscious (conscious being what you experience in the present moment; unconscious being everything else). It involves increasing your brain power by using your body's senses as filters for the information.

True development encourages individuals to apply these to their behaviour – that is, to apply what they have learnt. To ensure that the change continues, i.e. that a person has really *learned* from the training, the learning needs to pass from the short-term memory (STM) to the long-term memory (LTM). That way, learning passes from the conscious to the unconscious, and we become increasingly competent (and hopefully confident!) as a result.

Colin Rose (1985) has described the process of how learning is transferred from the STM to the LTM, using the MASTER method of Accelerated Learning. MASTER is an acronym:

Mindful state
Acquiring information
Sense
Trigger
Exhibit
Review

Mindful state

Before learning can take place, the students and the teacher all need to be *able* and *willing* to learn – that is, they have to have the *ability* to learn, and they must *want* to do so; everyone needs to be in a 'mindful state'.

The human brain has evolved into one of the most complex objects that we know about. It has an almost limitless capacity to process and work with information. Paul Maclean, a neurologist, developed the model of the 'Triune Brain' in 1949, which describes how instead of having one whole brain, our brains can be divided into three parts (*triune* means '3 brains in 1'). The three parts are: the reptilian (first brain), the limbic system, and the neo-cortex. The three parts carry out different functions.

The Triune brain

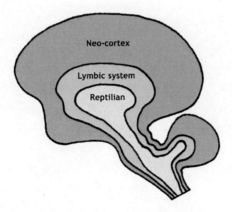

The *reptilian brain* is concerned with primitive physical functions – it controls muscles, balance and autonomic functions, such as breathing and our heartbeats. This part of the brain is active, even in deep sleep.

The *limbic system* is called the emotional brain and deals with emotions and short term memory. It is also involved in checking whether a situation is safe. If a situation is safe, then people can relax on an emotional level. The limbic system acts as a gateway to the third part – the neo cortex.

The *neo-cortex* is where our 'higher order' mind can be found; it deals with IQ, long-term memory and conscious reasoning.

To access the neo-cortex – where the long-term memory can be found, and therefore where what we have learned is stored – we need to ensure that the limbic system is comfortable with the teaching situation; we need to ensure a 'mindful state'.

Colin Rose describes how a mindful state can be achieved in three different ways:

a) Environment – you need to ensure that the learning environment is comfortable, safe and positive. This can be done through having plenty of natural light, comfortable seating, inclusive layout, gentle music, the use of colours, sounds, incense, candles etc. It can help to leave shoes outside the door as this helps to create a space separate from the 'outside world'.

b) 'I can, I will' – a positive attitude to the teaching experience will help in the learning process. Students can be encouraged to remember what their skills already are and their previous successes in learning. Asking students to think about what questions they have at the start can help to clarify uncertainties that may stop students feeling positive about how much they can learn.

c) Goals – it is important to know what these are. You can communicate your goals through providing pre-course information, as well as describing these at the start of a course. It is important for goals to appear to be realistic to students so that they can feel positive about what they can achieve. Your students will also have their own goals, and these you can check at the start of the course also.

Teacher Tips

1. At the start of the session, ask your students to draw a picture of themselves with the knowledge, skills and attitudes that they have now, and a picture of themselves with the knowledge, skills and attitudes that they would like to have at the end of the workshop. Alternatively, they can draw what a situation looks like to them at the start and then how it looks to them at the end of a workshop.

2. Use a 'Knowledge Tree'. Draw a large tree on the flipchart, and then turn the flipchart around so that students can't see it. Invite students to come to the chart, one by one, and place a dot, quickly draw a leaf, or stick a post-it-note where they feel they are on the tree. The higher that the student places their mark, the more knowledge or experience or confidence they feel that they have in relation to the subject of the course. At the end, show everyone the tree. You get a quick illustration of how comfortable your students are with the subject, and so you can adjust the pace and/or content of the learning opportunity accordingly. You can repeat the exercise at the end of the session, and compare the trees!

---

d) I would also, in my experience, add the importance of communicating clear principles in terms of expectations around behaviour during the learning opportunity. In traditional training models, this is called setting 'ground rules', which I find is a term that not everyone is comfortable with. You may have, or will develop, your own principles based on your attitudes, experiences, and the dynamics of the group. I have added in the following example of what I say at the start of any course, which might help you define your own principles, if you have not already done so.

Setting Principles – an example

'I always begin these sessions by clarifying a few principles that I work by, which I would just like to run through with you now.

1. First, I believe that we are all equals – that we are all students and teachers together. All I am doing is holding the space for you to develop, but I am learning too. You are my teachers as well as me being here as yours.

2. Secondly, all I can do here is share my experiences and my learning, which has led me to my Truth. I have learned only what I am ready to learn, based on my perception. I don't know the answers. I only know my answers; the ones my life has taught me; the ones I have been willing to learn from. In fact, my Truth changes as my learning and understanding develops. I am not an expert and I am not a guru. So on that basis, I don't ask that my Truth becomes your Truth.

   That means that I would like each of you to discern what resonates with you – if something I say feels helpful to you, then take it and use it in whatever way feels right for you. If something I say doesn't resonate, then that is perfect too – just let it go.

I ask that we maintain this with each other; that we check what resonates and what doesn't resonate with everything that each of us shares. None of us knows all the answers, all we can know is our own experience.

3. Thirdly, I am a spiritual being having a very human journey. This means I am still learning about who I am, what I am here to do, how I can make a difference. I am not "Buddha Enlightened". On my human journey, I still have meltdowns, I get cross with The Universe when I Don't Understand, I love watching South Park, and comedy swearing makes me giggle. I am, however, also committed to learning more about my own journey, including my shadow so I can come to a place of balance, unconditional love and compassion as quickly and easily as possible (and hopefully with some humour thrown in along the way ...!).

4. Fourthly, I may refer to some terms that we may all have different associations with. One of them is "God". For the benefit of everyone here, I mean God in a non-religious context, and will interchange the term with Goddess / the Divine / Source / the Creator – whatever feels right for you that reflects that "Higher Power" is what I mean.'

You can also invite students to offer any other principles that they would like to suggest for the course.

You might also use this as an opportunity to discuss any health and safety issues (fire escapes), domestic arrangements (lunch, breaks, location of toilets and kitchen) and describe the programme/course content itself.

Once students are in a mindful state, they are ready to start learning.

Acquiring information

Roger Sperry described in 1961 how the brain is divided into two halves – each half is called a 'hemisphere' (i.e. half a sphere). There is the left hemisphere and the right hemisphere, and they are joined by a bridge called the corpus callosum. Each hemisphere has different functions; the left hemisphere is concerned with logic, and the right with creative functions.

Once learners are in a mindful state, they are ready to accept and ingest new learning experiences. The teacher is able to present information in ways that encourage *whole-brain learning*.

Left: Logical	Right: Creative
Speech	Music
Maths	Emotion
Analytical thinking	Art
Reading	Patterns
Writing	Facial expressions
Evaluation	Colour
Logic	Whole pictures (holistic)
Rules	Intuition
HOW?	WHY?

Research has shown that our learning improves by 300% if BOTH sides of the brain work, not just one.

By stimulating BOTH sides of the brain, messages can link across the bridge, and the links get longer and stronger, and brain power and memory are strengthened.

A way to do this is to ensure that the senses are stimulated whilst using left-brain activities such as talking, thinking and learning. This can be done using colour pens, post-it notes, snacks, toys – anything to keep the mind active and working as a whole.

How we introduce the content of our teachings is a very important part of encouraging students to remember their experiences. An easy way to plan this is to use the 'Pyramid Technique'.

This technique guides you to say what you will say, say it, and say it again. For example, say 'I will be talking about the beauty of accepting yourself just as you are', then talk about the beauty of accepting yourself just as you are, and finish by saying 'we have just been talking about the beauty of accepting yourself just as you are'.

As for planning the actual content of your teaching, there are three things to remember: chunking, primacy and recency effects, and using the senses.

a) Chunking – the amount of information that the short-term memory can absorb is limited. Miller (1976) established that the brain can take in 7 plus or minus 2 chunks of information at any one time. That is, the brain prefers to receive between 5 and 9 chunks or 'bits' of information. Any more is too much. These are known as 'Miller's Magic Numbers': 7 ± 2. Another magic number is 3.

b) Primacy and recency effects – we tend to remember the first and last ideas more than the ones in between. This means that many short sessions are better than a single long one, because you will have more firsts and lasts. So, ensure that your exercises have lots of changes in them, and that your days have plenty of breaks.

c) Use the representational systems – this is how we use our senses to encode what we learn. Everyone has different preferences – some people are visual, some are auditory, others are kinaesthetic, and others still are digital.

Self-development exercise

You will find a copy of the Visual, Auditory, Kinaesthetic (VAK) Questionnaire in the Appendix, where you can assess your own preferred way of learning using your representational systems.

These preferences can change or evolve over time as we develop and our circumstances change, so you may wish to repeat this exercise every 6–12 months or so.

Different teaching methods appeal to different representational systems:

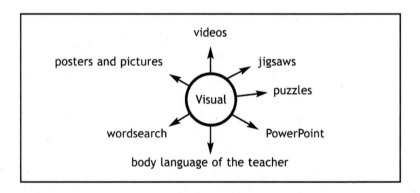

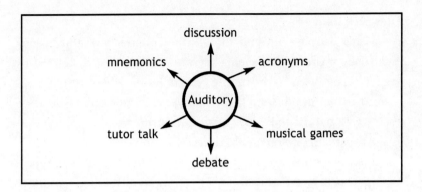

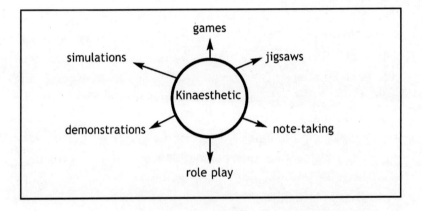

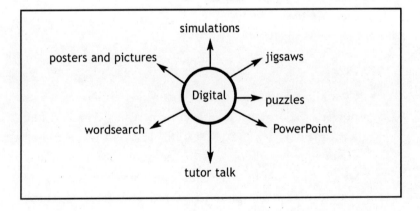

You can get a quick idea of what your students' preferred styles of learning are just by listening to what they say, and how they describe things.

Visual people will tend to describe colours, how things look etc. They memorise by seeing pictures and are less distracted by noise. They often have trouble remembering verbal instructions because their minds tend to wander. A visual person will be interested in what they SEE and LOOK at during your workshops.

An *auditory* person would describe sounds. They typically talk to themselves and are easily distracted by noise. They can repeat things back to you easily; they learn by listening. Auditory people like to be TOLD how they are doing. They will be interested in what you have to say when you are teaching.

A *kinaesthetic* person will describe feelings. They respond to physical rewards and touching as well as to exercises that focus on their emotions. They memorise by doing or experiencing something. They will be interested in what FEELS right during your teaching.

Digital people might give precise measurements. They may spend a fair amount of time talking to themselves. They like facts and scientific information. They will want to know if your teachings MAKE SENSE.

In addition to the teaching methods listed here, the senses can be further stimulated in every learning situation – helping us to learn more effectively.

1. Sight

- By adding colour to flipcharts and PowerPoint slides, the power of short-term memory increases by 75% and long-term memory by 25%. Be careful to avoid using red and green together (people with red-green colour blindness will not be able to differentiate between the colours, and people with dyslexia can find red and green together a barrier). Also, avoid using too many different colours on the same piece of flipchart paper – it can become distracting.

- Write as clearly as possible on a flipchart.
- Avoid using black and brown as your only colours on the flipchart – try to get a wider selection of colours that you can choose from. Always use the darker shades of those colours – these give a good contrast between the flipchart paper and the pen colour.
- Use illustrations. These don't have to be artistically amazing; in fact it can give your students something entertaining to laugh at if your drawings are artistically challenged (based on my own personal experience).
- Words linked to a picture will increase people's ability to remember facts as it means that the information is encoded in their memory on a dual basis, and builds a link between the right and the left brain.
- Sometimes when we are sitting still whilst on the phone, we can find ourselves doodling. This is an illustration of how using an additional sense, in this case sight, can help us with our concentration, so that we can listen and remember more easily.
- If you have a member of the audience who has a visual impairment, or is blind, it is important to verbally read aloud everything that you write on the flipchart – this is good practice to do with all audiences.

2. Smell
- Scent has a quicker, unfiltered access to the brain than any other sense. It raises awareness levels and attention dramatically.
- Scented pens and markers can help to achieve this efficiently.
- Aromatherapy is a wonderful way of supporting a powerful learning environment. Aromatherapy oils are extracts from certain plants and flowers that can help with balancing the nervous system, hormones and stress levels.

They can be used to relax, stimulate or uplift, depending on the mood that you wish to create. You can put a few drops in some pot pourri, or just leave 5–6 drops in a dish of warm water (for safety reasons don't burn it – it will slowly evaporate in the warm water anyway). Aromatherapy essential oils are pure and natural. Cheap imitations of oils do exist – these are called "perfume oils". Made with synthetic ingredients, perfume oils can cause migraines in some people, so do avoid using these as a cheaper substitute.

NB: Some stimulating aromatherapy oils are not suitable for pregnant women. Aromatherapist Christine Westwood advises that the following oils are not used with pregnant women: basil, clove, cinnamon, hyssop, juniper, marjoram, myrrh, sage and thyme. She also suggests using half the amount of the oils that you do use. Not every pregnant woman will know – or have shared – that she is pregnant, so it is wise to assume that you might have someone pregnant in your group when planning which oils to use. Mint and lemon are safe. Lemon is a strong mental stimulant – one study found that typing mistakes were reduced by 54% when lemon oil was distributed in the room. Pine is also helpful for grounding. Rose oil is wonderful for helping your students' hearts to open, but it is very expensive! Other oils that can be used include bergamot (calming), frankincense (calming), geranium (refreshing), orange (calming yet refreshing), grapefruit (antiseptic), neroli (calming but very expensive), and ylang-ylang (calming).

3. **Taste**
- Stimulate your students' taste buds by providing healthy snacks for them to eat – this helps to keep your teaching a memorable experience.

- You can use food as a reward, or as a means for dividing the large group into smaller groups for small-group work (e.g. 'If you select a red grape, you go into the "red group"; if you select a green grape, you go into the "green group"'). You could use nuts as an alternative. I would recommend avoiding anything too sugary as much as possible because of the sugar rush / crashes that can then happen, destabilising people's energies.
- Snacks also provide glucose to the brain very quickly, helping to maintain an energy supply, which it needs while it is working so hard ... and when working at high-energy frequencies (e.g. during meditation or healing work), your students will need extra calories and food to help them to cope with the amount of energy they are burning just through making those high-frequency connections.

4. Sound

- Choose music according to the mood you want to create (e.g. fast, upbeat music to energise a group; relaxing music to create an atmosphere for relaxed learning). Also consider the use of sound effects such as tapes of laughter to lighten an atmosphere.
- Meditation music is usually written at about 60 beats per minute. This pace emulates the pulse rate and puts the learner into a state where alpha rhythms in the brain predominate and the intake of information is exceptionally quick and easy. Other types of music (e.g. chillout dance) have the same pace, which you may prefer to use.
- Music charges and energises the brain. By 'accidentally' having a loud blast, you can wake a sleepy audience.
- If you have a member of your audience who is Deaf or hard of hearing, music can make it difficult for them to hear you or other people speaking, and so in these cases it

may not be possible to use music at the same time as you are talking. If you are aware that a participant may be Deaf, ask them beforehand what you can do to ensure that any barriers are removed as easily as possible. Also ensure that there is good lighting on your face so that it can be seen clearly for those who may be using lip-reading.

5. Touch

- Touch stimulates nerve endings near the skin surface that send messages to the brain – so providing stress balls, slinkies, lego, cards and crystals for delegates to play with during more passive sections of teaching keeps people energised and engaged.

Further considerations

a) Movement
- Movement stimulates the flow of blood and oxygen to the brain and helps people to stay more alert and energised – ensure that your teaching allows for people to move around, and include active exercises as well as mental exercises whatever subject you are teaching.
- Movement is also a very helpful and powerful means of grounding.
- You can use movement as a powerful reviewing tool. The majority of people represent the past to their left (to your right, as you are facing the audience). When putting completed flipcharts on the walls, put them up in chrono-logical order from 'the past' to 'the future'. Each time you review the teaching so far, stand on this side of the room (i.e. on your right), start from the beginning (the past), and slowly walk to the other side of the room (the present, the future). You are making links for your students between the learning materials, using time as the anchor.

b) Water

- The brain is 70% water, and regular rehydration helps it work – a 4–5% drop in water consumption results in 20–30% poorer concentration and performance.
- Water helps to facilitate the healing process energetically and physically by helping to flush out any toxins that need to be released. Often in spiritual teaching, healing is likely to be taking place, so always try to have water available if you can in teaching sessions.

There are more ways of stimulating any group so that they can get the most out of the teaching that you deliver and remember it more effectively for longer. Identify dry/tedious stuff and make it creative – above all, keep people actively involved on a regular basis.

Twenty minutes is the length of the average attention span – so try to change the pace and activity every 20 minutes at least.

The session after lunch tends to be the most challenging time for learning (when everyone goes to sleep). Try to keep people as active as possible for the first half-hour after lunch; then having a short break with cool drinks can help.

Once students have absorbed the information, the next step in the learning process is to make sense of the information.

Making Sense of it

Once we have acquired the information, we interpret it. To do this, we use our representational (sensory) systems:

- A *visual* person will need to have clear *images/pictures*

- An *auditory* person will need to have clear *discussion points* in mind
- A *kinaesthetic* person will need to have a clear idea of *how something works*
- A *digital* person will need to have facts and proof

The exercises that we use – the methods we apply as we design teaching opportunities – will influence how people make sense of what they are learning, according to their preferred learning styles.

This approach is summarised through the Learning Cycle devised by Kolb, Rubin and McIntyre (1974), which focuses on experiential learning. The Learning Cycle describes how an individual plans to experience something, has the opportunity to reflect upon that experience and then to develop a theory on how to proceed in the future, and then completes the cycle by doing what their theory suggests, thus initiating a new experience.

The most famous summary of 'learning styles' comes from the work of Honey and Mumford (1982), who identified the four styles of learning detailed below. The implications for teaching design are that we must seek to incorporate material that satisfies each of the learning styles, so that everyone – whatever their preference – has the opportunity to learn in a way that meets their needs effectively.

Learning Style	Approach	Learning Cycle
Activist	Those who are keen to have a go and get stuck in – sometimes without thinking	Do

Reflector	Those who are often quite cautions, who listen a lot, can be very self-critical and who think hard about experiences they have had	Reflect
Theorist	Those who are objective and enjoy working in an abstract way with ideas that are based upon their experience	Theorise
Pragmatist	Those who get a balance between coming up with ideas and putting them into practice	Plan

Traditionally, exercises are designed using the following approach:

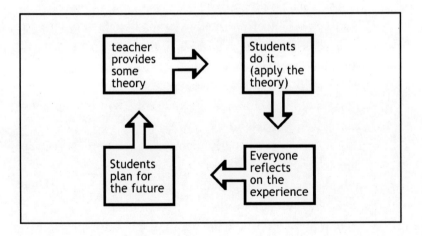

This approach, whilst useful, ensures that theorists are stimulated first, that activists then get to apply the information, reflectors have to wait until much later to have an opportunity to reflect, and the pragmatists have to wait later still.

As long as all types of learning styles are stimulated during the course, start individual exercises at different points in the cycle; start some exercises at the activist ('doing' stage), for example. That way, everyone maintains an interest.

Triggers

Triggers help to ensure that information in the memory can be easily accessed, when needed. The following all act as triggers:

- Mnemonics – a short rhyme, phrase, or other mental technique for making information easier to memorise (e.g. Never Eat Shredded Wheat, as a way of remembering North, East, South and West)
- Acronyms – a word formed from the initials or other parts of several words, (e.g. MASTER stands for something in this Handbook)
- Mind-maps – and other visual pictures
- Posters and pictures – participants will notice these throughout a teaching session
- Storytelling – particularly memorable, humorous, relevant stories
- Workbooks – these are documents that participants will take away with them
- Action plans – for how the learning will be applied
- Postcards – you could ask participants to complete a postcard with '3 things they would like to have changed within 3 weeks of the teaching', and you could post this to them 3 weeks after the event to remind them

- Logos – these are easily registered in the brain
- Certificates – again, documents that participants will take away with them, that will always remind students of their experiences and learning.

Exhibit

This is where the learning is illustrated through practice and exercises.

If small building blocks have been used at the A stage (Acquiring information), then the learning can be exhibited in small 'chunks' along the course, and in a more comprehensive way at the end of the teaching, depending on the length of the teaching!

Again, the exercises that encourage the exhibition of learning can be divided according to the representational systems:

- Visual
  - simulations
  - play/song/dance
  - demonstration
  - role play
  - practice
  - wordsearch
  - puzzles

- Auditory
  - discussions
  - role play
  - song/play/dance

- debate

- Kinaesthetic
  - alphabet game
  - play/song/dance
  - jigsaw
  - newsletter article

- Digital
  - debate
  - wordsearch
  - PowerPoint
  - tutor talk
  - puzzles
  - jigsaws

Once the participants feel confident in their ability to apply their learning, the whole process can be reviewed.

Review

It is important to review the learning that has taken place – and it needs to be done on a regular basis when it is first learned. However, a review only needs to take a couple of minutes.

Key questions that students need to ask themselves at this stage are:

a) What have I gained in terms of knowledge, skills and attitude?

b) What am I going to do with this?

c) Now I have arrived at this stage, what did I look/feel/ sound like when I look back to the start of the session?

The more the review work can fit into the whole range of the auditory, visual, kinaesthetic and digital learning preferences, the quicker the material is absorbed.

Teaching methods

There is a range of different methods that can be used to facilitate the learning process. Different methods appeal to individuals with different preferred learning styles, so it can benefit the whole group to use a variety of techniques.

1. Tutor talk / lecture

Often, this is a one-way presentation. Tutor talks allow the teacher to maintain some additional control over the material and the environment. They can be effective if they are structured around a theme, logically ordered, supported with examples and visual materials, not too long, properly paced and relevant. Improvements include intervals for discussion, asking questions, summarising and audience involvement.

2. Reading

This involves the students reading some material for themselves. Different people read at different speeds, and some people find it difficult to read and absorb information when doing it at the same time as other people; we can often be aware of whether we are reading 'quickly' or 'slowly' compared with others. This competition can be distracting. In order to help reinforce the learning, and make the exercise more interesting, it is helpful to add in time for discussions, summarising and more audience involvement.

3. Demonstration

This is where the teacher, or others, illustrates an idea, concept, or how to do a skill by doing it themselves in front of the group. This requires confidence and competence on the part of the teacher. It helps to break the demonstration into easy-to-digest chunks, so that students can learn using a step-by-step approach.

4. Note-taking

Students make notes about their learning in a way that is meaningful to them – on paper, or using a laptop or similar technological gadget. This is largely a question of personal choice and is dependent upon an individual's ability to organise their own learning.

5. Structured discussion

The teacher leads the discussion using a series of questions or statements that encourage students to explore a particular area of learning. This is useful for allowing all of the group to contribute and generate new ideas. Learning is generated from the participants rather than the teacher, and so can be empowering.

6. Brainstorming

Students come up with as many ideas as possible on a particular theme. These can then be noted visually using a flipchart. Brainstorming is often used to release creativity as part of a problem-solving exercise or discussion groups.

7. Case studies

Case studies help students to learn from examining and resolving a real-life situation that has been reduced to manageable proportions, without the risk involved in real life. Students study a situation or events and analyse possible solutions to problems they identify.

8. Team tasks / Group work
Groups work on tasks of a very general or specific nature. This can help to release pressure and also allows people who are quiet in larger group discussions to get involved. Group work encourages students to generate their own learning themselves.

9. Role play
Students re-enact situations by acting out certain behaviours or using certain skills to explore how they would do so in similar real-life situations.

10. Icebreakers/Games
These are useful at the beginning of events/days to introduce participants to each other, and to help them to relax and feel more comfortable about speaking in front of the group. They can create a positive and supportive atmosphere for the whole workshop, and are also useful throughout the training to 'revive' learners or help people relax after a particularly difficult session. For example, you can use a physical game after a long discussion or lecture.

11. Individual work/exercises
This enables students to reflect on their own experiences, needs, attitudes and skills. It can involve using question-naires, or creating something. perhaps using artwork, words or music. This can strongly support personal development and growth, and students often enjoy the time to focus on their own growth.

12. Guided meditations

This type of meditation enables learners to have their own experiences whilst the teacher guides them through the use of visualisation and relaxation techniques.

13. Silent/individual meditations

Again, learners are enabled to have their own experiences, as the leader invites them to be relaxed whilst being in their own 'space'. Some people find meditating on their own very difficult so they may need an introduction or some guidance in how to do so.

14. Coaching

Coaching empowers an individual to reflect upon their own situation and enables them to decide what actions they will take to make changes to their situation. It often occurs in one-to-one situations, even when you are in front of a larger group (i.e. in a teaching situation).

Now that we have explored how we learn psychologically and cognitively, using 'whole-brain learning', we can look at the impact of learning – and change – on our energetic bodies, and what this means for us as Spiritual Teachers.

Energetic Learning

Newtonian and Quantum principles

We will begin this chapter by considering how energy works – by beginning with the smallest unit of energy known to us: the atom.

An atom is a basic unit of matter – the word comes from the Greek *atomos* which means 'uncuttable'. It is made up of subatomic particles; neutrons and protons are tightly packed together in a nucleus, whilst electrons flow in energy fields around the nucleus.

- A neutron carries a neutral charge
- A proton carries a positive charge
- An electron carries a negative charge

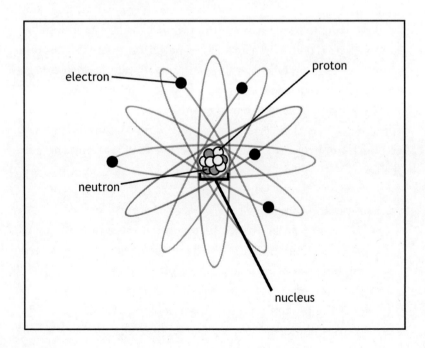

There is a lot of 'empty space' between the nucleus and the energy fields that carry the electrons. In fact there is so much space within atoms – and atoms cluster together to make matter – that, as Marcus Chown describes in his book *Quantum Theory Cannot Hurt You*, 99.9% of the volume of ordinary matter is empty space. If all of it was condensed, you could fit the entire human race into the volume of a sugar cube!

There are two main types of physics – Newtonian physics and Quantum physics.

Newtonian physics is the physics many of us learned about at school – it is all about gravity. Gravity is a natural phenomenon that gives weight to objects. Tom Kenyon gives a simple example of how we could easily explain the difference between these two schools of physics. He states that if an object is larger than 1000th of an inch, it is big enough to have a gravitational field. This is the branch of physics that lets us calculate the distance an object (e.g. a ball) will travel if we know the mass and the forces applied to that object.

According to Kenyon, quantum physics governs anything that is less than 1000th of an inch. It is based on quanta – discrete chunks of Light. These are so small and vibrate at such a high frequency that we can't see them using our physical eyes.

Quantum physicists have scientifically proved that Light (photons) behaves in certain interesting ways – an understanding of which can help to explain our experiences of working energetically:

- A photon can behave like a wave or a particle
- A photon can be in two places at the same time (like you being in England and Canada at the same time!) – indeed photons can be in thousands of places at once
- The moment you try to look at a photon and study it, it is as if the photon knows you are looking at it and it disappears – photons don't like being observed!

- Waves of light can penetrate apparently impenetrable barriers
- Photons and indeed all particles are connected to each other – a change to the behaviour of one photon affects the behaviour of other photons ('entanglement theory')

We are said to live in a Newtonian and Quantum world *at the same time*, in terms of how we learn. Kenyon further describes how the two worlds meet in our mind – in the synapses in our brains which is where matter (in particular tiny chemicals called neurotransmitters) becomes too small to have a gravitational field. And so our learning – our thoughts – occur energetically, not just in our physical brains.

When we experience learning, it can lead to change. We can measure this change physically using the Newtonian approach in terms of our behaviour in our material world – or we can view that change as occurring through our thoughts in the Quantum world. Our thoughts and intentions involve creating changes energetically. This can result in growth and development energetically, which may be experienced as energetic healing in our chakras, or aura, or through time. This energetic healing can also lead to physical changes in a way that brings us back 'full circle' – to demonstrating changes in our physical reality.

Dr David Hamilton, a pharmacologist who has researched the power of thought and the impact that it has on the human body, describes some interesting research on this in his book *How Your Mind Can Heal Your Body*. He documents many experiments and research trials that have shown how the power of thought can lead to physical changes and healing in the body. For example, he describes research that has shown that children's wounds heal more quickly when covered with a plaster with a picture of a cartoon character on it, rather than a plain plaster. He suggests this is because the children focus more on how the plaster is helping the wound because they like looking at the plaster. Other research has demonstrated how muscles can become more physically developed just by imagining yourself exercising them – without you lifting a finger! He further describes truly amazing examples of people who have literally changed the state of bone, and cured themselves of terminal or 'incurable' cancers – all with the power of thought.

In spiritual teaching, we are often working on both the Quantum and the Newtonian level simultaneously.

Through these gateways between the Newtonian and Quantum worlds, we enter one of the ways that we are described as existing energetically – the aura; this is an energy field that is said to surround our physical body. As well as learning affecting our brain development, and our behaviour, all learning opportunities may also lead to the development of our energetic selves through our auras and chakras.

The aura

The aura is a general term that describes several layers of high-frequency energy combined. Our auras can be photographed using Kirlian photography.

Etheric body – This is the layer closest to the physical body. Some people perceive it as blue. It contains the template for the physical body. If the etheric body is out of balance, then the physical body will be also. For example, following shock or trauma, our etheric body is said to move to one side of us to protect us from immediately experiencing the full impact of the trauma. It takes 4–6 weeks to return – about the time for someone to start to really feel the impact of the experience. (Said to be connected to the root chakra.)

Emotional body – This extends 4–6 inches away from the etheric body. This is where we store our emotions, and can

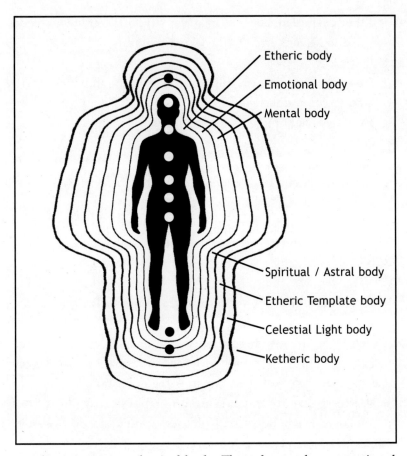

Etheric body
Emotional body
Mental body
Spiritual / Astral body
Etheric Template body
Celestial Light body
Ketheric body

also impact our physical body. The colours of our emotional body change as our emotions change. (Said to be connected to the sacral chakra.)

Mental body – This can be yellow or blue in colour, and holds our thought processes. The more active we are in our thinking, the brighter the colour is said to be. (Said to be connected to the solar plexus chakra.)

Spiritual/astral body – This layer is said to connect our physical and higher bodies, and our physical and spiritual experiences. It can be a multitude of colours. (Said to be connected to the heart chakra.)

Etheric template body – This layer supports our etheric body. (Said to be connected to the throat chakra.)

Celestial Light body – This is the layer through which we are said to communicate with spirit. (Said to be connected to the third-eye chakra.)

Ketheric template – Golden bright light, which is believed to protect us. (Said to be connected to the crown chakra.)

When we learn, that learning may lead to changes through all aspects of ourselves – physically, mentally, emotionally, energetically and spiritually.

How we receive information energetically

As we have already discovered in the chapter on Accelerated Learning, we use our senses to receive information that we can use to learn. Psychological theories focus on how we use our senses to receive information from our physical world for our psychological, emotional and physical growth. We do use our senses in other ways too, however. We can receive information about our world energetically.

Our senses operate not just physically but energetically too. For some very developed intuitive people, there is not much of a difference between how they experience their intuitive or energetic reality compared with their physical reality. However, for most of us, there is a clear difference between how we receive information through our senses in the energetic world compared with the physical world.

The following terms describe how energetic information is received:

- Clairvoyance (*clair* is French for 'clear', *voir* is French for 'to see' – as in 'voyeur'; so clairvoyance means 'clear seeing')

- Clairaudience (clear hearing)
- Clairsentience (clear feeling)
- Claircognisance (clear thinking)
- Clairalliance (clear smelling)
- Clairgustant (clear tasting)

In other words, we receive energetic information through our senses – it is our senses that 'read' what is happening in the energetic world and allow us to experience it.

Self-development exercise

You will find a copy of the Divine Communication questionnaire in the Appendix, where you can assess your own preferred way of receiving energetic information.

These preferences can change or evolve over time as we develop and our circumstances change, so you may wish to repeat this exercise every 6-12 months or so.

There are strong similarities between the VAK and Divine Communication descriptions:

- Clairvoyance could be said to be linked to visual learning preferences
- Clairaudience could be said to be linked to auditory learning preferences
- Clairsentience could be said to be linked to kinaesthetic learning preferences
- Claircognisance could be said to be linked to digital (thinking) learning preferences

---

Self-development question
Were your VAK and Divine Communication Questionnaire findings similar? This is likely – the more strongly we use a sense physically, the more likely we are to receive through it energetically because we are comfortable learning through it.

Chakras

In this section, I will very briefly describe the core chakras. This is not intended as a comprehensive guide; it is a general introduction. For more information on chakras, I would recommend any of the books by Anodea Judith, who relates the functions of chakras to our physical, mental, emotional and spiritual health.

What are chakras?
Chakra is a Sanskrit word which means 'wheel', and is often associated with the turning of a wheel.

Carl Jung referred to the chakras as the 'gateways of consciousness'. Each chakra is said to be a wheel-like vortex of pure energy that is associated with a specific realm of the human experience. Chakras flow through all four bodies – the physical, emotional, mental and spiritual – spinning at great speed.

Traditionally, there were considered to be 7 major chakras, although more recently, awareness has developed about the *new chakras*. There are different schools of thought about how many there are, some focusing on 12 chakras, others up to 36 and more.

I will summarise 8 chakra centres here; the 7 traditionally taught and the '8th chakra', also known as the 'higher heart' chakra.

A note on the colours and sounds of chakras: Each chakras is considered traditionally to have a particular colour and sound associated with it. For example, the heart chakra is said to be green in colour and to resonate with the musical note 'F'. This is because the energy that flows through each chakra is said to resonate with a particular frequency, which can always be seen as a colour and heard as a sound.

In my experience, and in the increasing experiences of others, the frequency of energy flowing through each chakra is changing regularly, and so the same colours and sounds can no longer be associated with each chakra. This is said to be happening because our energy bodies are increasingly vibrating at faster and faster frequencies, as our consciousness is rising. So not only are chakra colours changing, but they are also different for different people, and can change on a regular basis; for example, a person's heart chakra could be green one day, gold the next, platinum the day after! You can find out more about the colours of your own chakras by connecting to them through meditation.

Each colour has meanings associated with them which you can find out more about in the section on 'Energy and colour', and which may help you to understand more about what is happening to each of your chakras as they resonate at newer energy frequencies.

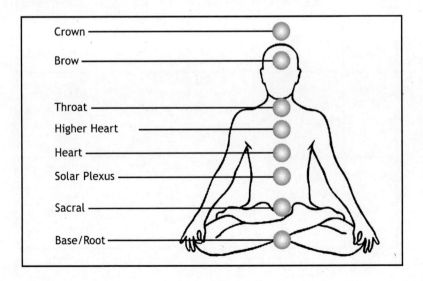

Crown
Brow
Throat
Higher Heart
Heart
Solar Plexus
Sacral
Base/Root

Chakra	Physical	Emotional	Mental	Spiritual
Crown	Central nervous system	Life and death	Wisdom	'Being'
Third Eye	Brain, eyes, nose and ears	Maturity	Trusting intuition	Awareness of 'being'
Throat	Throat	Expressing oneself	Communi-cation	Speaking one's own Truth
Higher Heart	Thymus gland (immune system)	Compassion	Under-standing	Healing across time
Heart	Heart and circulation	Uncondi-tional love for self and others	Healing fear-based emotions	Trust
Solar Plexus	Digestive system	Self-esteem	Creativity	Connects soul and ego
Sacral	Reproductive system and kidneys	Relation-ships with others / Passion	Addictions	Giving and receiving emotions
Base / Root	Sexuality and rectum	Lust	Safety	Connecting to the Earth and material life

Energy and colour

We are all energetically made up of atoms and photons that vibrate at different energy frequencies. Each energy frequency appears as a colour and a sound. We prefer different colours at different times in our lives. The colour that we like least, we tend to avoid looking at, and we will also avoid wearing clothes or eating foods of that colour. We are composed of all energy frequencies, and so rejecting any particular colour can lead us to fall out of balance energetically.

A lovely way to rebalance energetically is to do so using colour, by checking each day what your least favourite colours are and then trying to connect with them. You can wear those colours, look at them more, eat or drink them in some way. A simple way of checking is to get a pack of 10–12 felt pens or crayons and arrange them in order of preference every morning from your most favourite to your least favourite. Once you have identified which colours are your least favourite on that day, you can use the chart below to identify what aspects you are perhaps in need of healing.

There are many different colour-healing systems that describe what a colour can tell us about where we are emotionally, physically, mentally and spiritually.

The following chart draws on the wisdom of a colour-healing system called Aura-Soma®. It was channelled by a pharmacist called Vicky Wall. Aura-Soma® uses colour, plant (flower and herb), animal and mineral energies to support healing and wellbeing in all ways. It describes what each colour is said to correspond to according to this system. Aura-Soma® focuses more on the energetic and emotional aspects of colour; however, I felt it might be helpful to add physical information in too.

If you already work with colour, and would interpret the colours in a different way from that described below, I would suggest that you continue to work with what you know. I believe that we are always shown what we need to see based on how we would interpret the information ourselves. So, for example, I might interpret one meaning from the colour green because I connect with Aura-Soma© ... but another person might interpret something else from the same colour based on the knowledge that they have. Each, I feel, would be right for the person receiving it. I feel the same principles apply when working with symbols too.

Colour	Physical	Emotional	Mental	Spiritual
Blue	Thyroid and throat	Nurturing and calm	Communication and leadership	Peace and protection
Yellow	Liver, skin, and central nervous system	Joy, happiness and fear	Knowledge, intellect and indecisiveness	Individual will
Red	Blood and circulation	Passion, anger and courage	Extraversion and separateness from others	Awakening
Green	Heart, lungs and thymus	Openness, generosity, jealousy	Boundaries with self and others; balance	Seeking truth, healing, compassion
Orange	Intestines, spleen and gall bladder	Bliss, wisdom and shock	Decision making and dependency	Insight
Violet	Mucus-producing cells, skull	Sensitivity and grief	Humility and contemplation	Spirituality, healing, and service

Royal Blue	Eyes, ears, nose and pineal gland	Objectivity, neutrality and depression	Intuition	Higher mind functions and clarity through senses
Turquoise	Heart, throat and thymus gland	Empathy and optimism	Media / new communi-cations and teaching	Healing through time
Olive	Gall bladder, large intestine and lungs	Self-love and leadership	Harmony and completion	Clarity about one's path
Gold	Spine and skin	Deep joy/ ecstacy, desire, peace	Wisdom, self-righteousness	Enlighten-ment, trans-mutation
Coral	Glands, elimin-ation and sexual organs	Uncon-ditional love for self	Inter-dependence/ cooperation, projection and self-analysis	Higher intuition
Magenta	Repro-ductive and hormonal systems	Love in all things, giving often more than receiving	Perfectionism	Divine love

'Black' does not truly exist in nature. What we perceive as black is said to be a very very very dark version of another colour. For example, in Aura-Soma®, that very very dark colour is experienced as deep magenta. Clothes that are made of synthetic dyes will be what we know as 'black'. 'Black' (or its equivalent in nature) is a very important colour – it absorbs all other colours before individual colours are identified. It is the colour of the womb and of creation.

White reflects all colours, so beams back what people need for themselves.

Teacher Tips – how you can work with colour to help your students

There are several ways in which you can support the development of your students through your use of colour.

Notice what colours your students will be looking at in the venue, and worn by you – they will see these colours a lot during the time of your teaching. Lighter shades tend to be more calming. If students spend a lot of time, for example, looking at something red, it may bring out their anger, whereas looking at the colour blue may help them to feel more at peace. Orange can be a good colour if people are healing a lot of emotional issues, although it might be strong for some people. Green is great for maintaining clear boundaries between you, as well as helping all to be more in their own Truth. Coral is a very good colour for encouraging students to focus on loving themselves. You can use the previous colour chart to help you decide what type of atmosphere you would like to create.

1. Notice the colours in the venue (this can include the walls, floor coverings and paintings)
2. Be conscious of the colours that you choose to wear
3. Choose lunches that include food colours that you would like people to eat more of
4. Print handouts on pastel-coloured paper
5. Provide colour pens for students to write with
6. Refer to colours in guided visualisations

Energy and sound

In the same way that each colour is an expression of a particular energy frequency, each energy frequency is also expressed as a sound (or tone).

Whenever we create a sound, we can often – if we are still – *feel* the vibration of that sound and where it is reflected in our bodies.

Stewart Pearce teaches about the importance of communicating and speaking via one's heart. He describes how, often, most of us speak at a tone (or note) that connects us to our throat, or above (e.g. our mind) – particularly when we are anxious. He gives powerful examples of what happens when we lower our tone of voice so that it resonates at the same frequency as our heart.

Once we are speaking with the same tone that resonates from our heart, we are more easily able to connect with, and bring through, communication that reflects our own Truth, strength and power. Speaking at a higher tone is more likely to be connecting with the mind, which is often a source of a lot of mental activity that can lead to fear and anxiety.

When we speak from our own heart sound, we are able to speak from a place that is calmer, safer, softer yet stronger and so more influential. And when we speak from our hearts, others can feel it in their hearts – which adds to the power of it.

Stewart Pearce has given the example of the power and influence of US President Barack Obama. During his election, he was able to gather significant levels of support from voters. Of course there will have been many possible reasons for this, including political reasons to do with the waning popularity of his predecessor and his predecessor's policies. If you listen to Barack Obama speak, however, he clearly speaks using the tone that resonates through his heart, and the power he is able to communicate with can feel strong and influential.

I have joked with my students that it is a bit like 'using The Force' as described in *Star Wars*. There is a scene in the first original film (film number 4, *A New Hope*) where Obi Wan Kenobi speaks to a Storm Trooper who is about to prevent him and Luke Skywalker from entering Mos Eisley Space Quadrant on Tatooine, where they eventually meet Han Solo. The following discussion takes place, during which Obi Wan uses the power of 'The Force' and speaks from his heart to put the Storm Trooper into a trance so that he then does what Obi Wan tells him to:

Storm Trooper (pointing to Luke Skywalker): 'Let me see his identification'
Obi Wan: 'You don't need to see his identification'
Storm Trooper: 'We don't need to see your identification'
Obi Wan: 'These aren't the droids you are looking for'
Storm Trooper: 'These aren't the droids we are looking for'
Obi Wan: 'He can go about his business'
Storm Trooper: 'You can go about your business'
Obi Wan: 'Move along'
Storm Trooper: 'Move along'

Luke Skywalker and Obi Wan then continue their journey uninterrupted.

I feel that speaking from one's heart – using one's heart sound – is a bit like using 'The Force'. As a teacher, by speaking from the heart, you can help your students to connect more with the energy of their heart – and through this help them come to a place of greater peace, calm, safety, openness, empowerment, strength and their Truth. Also, your students respond more to you and your teaching – it helps to bring you to your Truth, peace, strength and power too.

Self-development exercise – finding your heart sound

Make an 'aaaahh' sound or hum aloud at any tone or note that you wish to use. Place your hand, palm facing you, about 3 inches in front of your mouth. Move your hand up and down in front of your chakras, and feel for where that tone is causing a vibration in your energy.

If the vibration is above your heart, then lower the tone of the sound you are making. Move your hand down too, so you can locate where the vibration is moving to.

If the vibration is below your heart, then raise the tone of the sound you are making. Move your hand up too, so you can locate where the vibration is moving to.

Continue this process until you are making a sound that is creating a vibration in front of your heart chakra. Practise speaking using this tone regularly.

Teaching Skills for Spiritual Teachers

In this chapter, we will explore some of the many skills that we use as Spiritual Teachers, including presenting information, communication, facilitation and channelling. As with all skills, we can all continue to develop through reflection and practice. This chapter is adapted from the Training for Trainers course I used to facilitate at the National Union of Students.

What are the benefits for students when they attend a course or workshop, as opposed to reading the information in a book?

- It gives students an opportunity to learn as they experience you presenting information and communicating in person with the audience
- Interactive and exciting – definitely not passive
- Gives lots of information very quickly
- Combines learning preferences (e.g. visual and auditory)
- Teacher can adapt content to the needs of the group and personalise the session
- Teacher can adjust the pace of the session to the group
- Allows audience to ask questions and check points
- Encourages creative thinking – people bouncing ideas off one another
- Teacher can measure the understanding of the group by asking questions.
- Learning is absorbed more effectively – by using different techniques that stimulate the senses
- Learning happens on many levels
- Students get to see the 'bigger picture'
- Collectively raises energies, so all benefit from more powerful learning/healing

- Opportunity to meet other people
- Enthusiasm on the part of the teacher can encourage and motivate students
- *Inspiring* teachers can *inspire* students
- Multidimensional learning opportunity (books can be very one-dimensional)
- Fun – there is the personal touch (the human element)

Self-development questions

Think of some of your own learning experiences in terms of the presentation / delivery of the courses or workshops.

Where you attended inspirational courses, what did the teacher(s) do to engage, inspire and empower you in terms of their communication with the audience, and how they presented the content?

Where you felt less inspired, what did the teacher(s) do in terms of their communication with the audience and how they presented the content that did not resonate with you so much?

What can you learn from these experiences to empower you to develop your skills further?

Presentation skills

As teachers, we use presentation skills to communicate information to an audience. Presenting involves two aspects in particular; the way that the teacher presents themselves, and how the content is presented.

The following factors are important in terms of how we, as teachers, deliver and present:

- Being fully prepared with materials and equipment

- Being mindful of personal appearance and presentation (appropriately dressed for the audience) – this includes personal hygiene!
- Delivering and communicating in a way that is clear and concise
- Punctuality / time management
- Keeping to the point
- Presenting charismatically
- Being enthusiastic
- Appearing calm and confident (even if you don't feel it!)
- Easily communicating your knowledge and understanding
- Smiling
- Having a sense of humour
- Communicating in a warm and approachable manner
- Being self-aware – not too much fidgeting that can distract students
- Holding (not controlling) the space
- Finding out what the group already knows (it is helpful to start by assuming nothing)
- Stopping for questions regularly
- Being fully present
- Avoiding the use of jargon and technical terminology – or when using it, explaining it first
- Involving students actively (for example, by asking questions)
- Looking for feedback to check the group's understanding and any further needs
- Voice quality – speaking from your heart chakra as much as possible, and using a positive and encouraging tone of voice
- Communicating articulately
- Making eye contact
- Using positive, welcoming and open body language

The following factors are important in terms of how we deliver and present the content of the course:

- Being interactive – using games, tasks, icebreakers
- Familiarity with content
- Having a clear introduction, including communicating about expectations and principles
- Presenting it in easy-to-digest 'chunks'
- Stimulating the audience through all senses – providing balance and variety for all learning styles
- Making sure the content is engaging
- As a teacher, obviously enjoying the content because of your belief in the subject
- Using the Pyramid Technique (saying what you are going to say, saying it, then saying it again), e.g. say 'I will be talking about the beauty of accepting yourself just as you are', then talk about the beauty of accepting yourself just as you are, and finish by saying 'We have just been talking about the beauty of accepting yourself just as you are.' This ensures your message is reinforced – and so you increase the potential recall for your audience.
- Providing helpful and accessible materials, such as handouts, that students can take away with them
- Arranging the room to suit the group – with plenty of light, air and space for people to move around in when possible
- Using plenty of music, images, candles, crystals, toys, fragrances, instruments etc.
- Good health and safety awareness – taping down cables and removing all obstacles, for example

We have considered the importance of presentation skills, as a way of providing information to your audience. Now we will consider how that information is communicated to others.

Communication skills

The root of the word 'communication' comes from the Latin for 'sharing' – *communico*. Other similar words include: commune, common, community, commitment, commonality.

Communication can be said to be the sharing or exchange of information. It helps us all to gain understanding. Communication can be verbal and non-verbal. Verbal communication involves sound – especially tone of voice – to convey that exchange of information. Non-verbal communication includes body language, the content of the message itself (i.e. the words used), eye contact, physical touch, emails and written communication, and also includes sign language.

Albert Mehrabian is Professor Emeritus of Psychology at the University of Los Angeles, California (UCLA). He has been researching the role of communication since the 1960s. He found that when someone is communicating an attitude or feeling, the effectiveness of the message could be broken down in the following way:

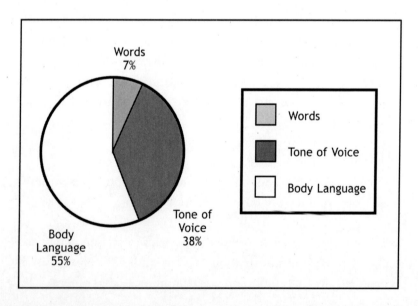

Professor Mehrabian also found that when we do not believe what is being conveyed to us, we choose to trust the non-verbal communication more than the verbal. In other words, we can tell if someone is sincere and honest in their communication not by the words that they use, but by the body language and tone of voice that they use to convey the message.

We will consider how it is that we communicate with our body and tone of voice when we consider all of the skills that teachers use to deliver courses and workshops. We will now consider how we give and receive messages as part of the Cycle of Communication.

The Cycle of Communication

This is a breakdown of how we communicate.

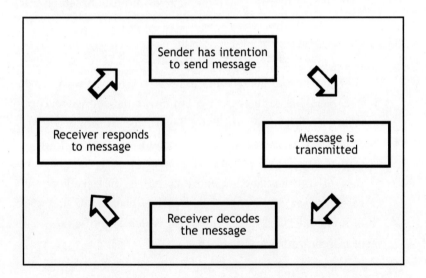

1. *Sender intends to send a message* – the objectives and purpose behind sending the message are important factors in how that message is then transmitted.

    For example, if the intention is to inspire others, the message is likely to then be transmitted in a loving way. If the intention of the sender is to make themselves feel more powerful than another, they will then transmit the message using their body language and tone of voice in a way that tries to assert their authority.

2. *The message is transmitted* – using speech, body language, using a letter or an email etc.

3. *The receiver decodes the message* – depending on their knowledge, beliefs, attitudes, cultural experiences, what they were taught as children at home and with their peers.

   In effect, the message receiver breaks down the meaning of the message according to their world view. This is where miscommunications are most likely to occur; each of us will interpret a message differently based on our own individual experiences and views. So even if the sender's intention is to send a message lovingly, it might be interpreted differently by the receiver.

   There are other factors that affect how the receiver decodes a message; in particular, how balanced we feel and how effectively we are listening. If, for example, we are distracted in any way – through hunger, tiredness, disinterest, stress, other thoughts – we can only then receive part of the message. In these cases, as the receiver only receives *part* of the message that has been sent, they can only decode part of the message, which amplifies the risk of miscommunications further.

   An additional challenge for the receiver occurs when decoding a written message – particularly in email form. This is because there is an absence of the sender's tone of voice or body language to communicate the attitude and feelings of the sender. This is another source of miscommunications: relying on assumptions based on what you feel or think you might know of a person, or how you expect others to communicate with you, to help you interpret the message.

4. *The receiver responds to the message that they have received* – this is where the receiver sends a message back to the sender, thus becoming the sender. The original sender receives feedback that enables them to establish if their message was understood as they intended for it to be understood.

    The same difficulties can arise with how messages are sent and received as have been already described, as the cycle of communication continues.

Having considered the communication cycle, we will now explore some of the skills that we use to communicate – in particular, listening skills, asking questions and giving and receiving feedback.

Listening skills

Listening is the means by which we understand the messages that are verbally given to us. Listening is more than just hearing; hearing is the process of the ears receiving sound whereas listening is the process of the brain attaching meaning to the sound.

Why is it important that, as teachers, we listen to the messages that our students are sending to us?
Reasons can include the following:

- We can establish the needs of students – then we can use this information to create as safe, relaxing and positive a learning environment as possible
- We can identify their expectations in terms of how they would like to learn and develop, and tailor our workshop

accordingly
- We can check the understanding of students
- Effective listening can help our students to feel valued
- When we listen effectively, we gain a greater understanding of the perspective of our students. Then we can respond more accurately to their feedback – which can increase the power and influence of what we are communicating
- We can become aware of potential difficulties more quickly

Barriers to listening

The following factors can make it difficult for us to listen effectively:

- Feeling uncomfortable (hungry; thirsty; needing the toilet; too cold; too hot; feeling tired; using an uncomfortable chair or being in an uncomfortable learning environment)
- Being distracted by other sounds / the view out of the window
- Being distracted by your own thoughts running through your head
- Feeling bored or disinterested
- Feeling anxious
- Believing that you know what the other person is going to say before they have finished
- Disagreeing with another person's message
- Having an emotional response to another person's message – even if you are able to hold back from showing it
- Finding it difficult to physically hear what someone else is saying
- Different accents that you are not used to
- Feeling out of balance energetically
- Being ungrounded

> **Self-development questions**
> What prevents you from listening effectively to others?
> What can you do to make it easier for yourself to listen effectively?
> How do you demonstrate effective listening to others?

How we demonstrate effective listening

- Eye contact
- Nodding
- Smiling
- Using utterances at appropriate places, e.g. murmurs like 'uh huh'
- Inviting further contributions (e.g. 'Can you tell us/me more about that?')
- Repeating back key points of what has been said
- Paraphrasing – summarising what someone has communicated to you and saying this to them (e.g. 'If I understand correctly, you are asking/saying ...')
- Asking questions

Asking questions

The types of questions that we ask can be summarised using the following three main categories: 'open', 'closed' and 'ones to avoid'.

Open questions

These encourage the other person to give an answer in detail – helping the student to explore their thoughts and feelings in more detail. The student can therefore be more actively involved in their own learning. For example:

'How do you feel about …?'
'What do you think would happen if …?'
'Why do you think that …?'

Closed questions

These questions can help you to check your students' under-standing. They can also limit the students' response – and so may be a useful way of intervening with someone who may be talking a lot. Closed questions include 'yes/no' questions, and those that have one-word or short answers. For example:

'Did you read that book?'
'Do you understand?'
'Do you need more time?'

Questions to avoid

Any question that confuses, misleads, or unnecessarily discourages someone from talking is unhelpful. Asking a large number of questions in one go can also be difficult for others, because they don't know which question to answer first, and can forget some that have been asked. For example:

'I assume that you all know about this?'
'You can't believe that?'
'What do you mean? You did say that you had done this before?'

Teacher Tip – responding to questions to which you do not know the answer

Irrespective of how prepared you might be, how well read, how experienced you are, you will always come across situations where you do not know the answer to a question

---

that you are asked.

I would suggest using one or either of these approaches, on their own, or combined:

1. Be honest, and say 'I don't know.' You can go further and offer to find out. You can also ask if any other student knows the answer – this approach really honours your students as your equals. Also, students really respect the integrity and honesty of you saying 'I don't know' much more than you trying to pretend that you know more than you do.

   It is also very liberating and empowering for you, as a teacher. It can take the pressure off you if you are able to recognise that you can't and will never know the answer to everything – all you can ever do is your best!

2. Deflect the question back to your students. You can ask if anyone else knows the answer. Again, this engages your students as equals, and can help you to find out what your students know, so you can tailor your teaching accordingly.

As well as listening to our students, and asking the right questions, we need to let them know that they are on the right track. Feedback skills are a vital communication skill that teachers use to let other people know that they are developing and learning, or if there are misunderstandings or difficulties. We will now consider the giving of feedback.

Giving feedback

1. **Positive feedback is highly motivating**

   Praise specific actions that students have done well to encourage and motivate the person to keep developing.

'That's a great suggestion', 'That has worked really well', 'You have described that situation really clearly, thank you'.

2. **Focus on the behaviour, not the person**

   Give someone feedback based on 'how they have acted' not 'what they are'. It is important not to focus on someone's personality, but on their behaviour.

   'How do you think your reading could be more empowering?' (in a psychic development class), *not* 'You are not very good at making people feel empowered.'

3. **Be specific, not general**

   If you give examples of specific situations that your students can refer to, they have the choice of using that information in a more helpful way.

   'You may need more information about this subject', *not* 'Sometimes you seem confused'.

4. **Report feelings or consequences of behaviour**

   What a person's actions make you feel is valid feedback for both of you; you are given a reflection of something in you that may need healing, and they are showing some aspect through which they might further evolve.

   'When you communicate in that loving way, I feel more positive about myself, and this makes me want to make even more positive changes in my life.'

5. **Be timely**

   In general, feedback is most useful at the earliest opportunity after the given behaviour (depending on the person's readiness to hear it, how ready you are to communicate from a place of unconditional love, whether there is support available from others etc.).

6. **Remember that the person you are giving feedback to has feelings**

   Try to empathise with their perspective, and how they might feel with the feedback that you are giving them.

7. **Be open to receiving feedback as part of a two-way dialogue**

   You will also receive feedback from your students. Always acknowledge the feedback by saying 'Thank you' – even if it is difficult feedback to receive. Avoid justifying, defending or denying the feedback – just ask the person for more information; this may be a developmental opportunity for you too.

We will consider receiving feedback more in the chapter on Self-Development.

So far in this chapter, we have considered a range of teaching skills, including presentation, communication, listening, questioning and feedback skills. We use all of these skills to *deliver* our teaching. As Mehrabian found, the most important way that we deliver our teaching and communicate with our students is by using our body language and our tone of voice. In effect, we are *performing* to help us to deliver a learning opportunity.

I always think it is a little bit like being an actor – when we accentuate key aspects of our messages by using more energy and enthusiasm (without being over the top!), we make it easier for others to be energised by the experience.

Posture and body language

- When standing, be in a relaxed position, legs straight and slightly apart, shoulders back and head up. Face your students; this makes you appear relaxed and confident.

- Avoid hunching your shoulders, hiding behind a flipchart, or moving too much. This will make you seem anxious and distract the audience from what you are saying.
- If you are sitting, again sit up straight, relaxed, with your shoulders back and head up. Again, do face your students.
- Crossing your arms or legs can suggest defensiveness. It can look as though you are protecting yourself from your students, which emphasises a feeling of separation between you and them. Sitting too casually or turning away from your students suggests a lack of interest on your part.
- If you are working with a very small group, avoid leaning forward too much or being too close to the students as you might make the group feel intimidated and uncomfortable. Always be aware of other people's space and respect their boundaries.
- Use effective hand movements that help to stress the valuable and important ideas.
- Avoid using your hands in a fidgety way to relax you; either by fiddling with a pen or blu-tack, or by stroking your head or hair. This is also distracting and is a sign of nervousness.
- Smile at appropriate moments, particularly before you begin to speak.

Voice

The way you use your voice will give out messages as much as your body language and the content of what you say. As we discussed earlier, the greatest power in using your voice comes when speaking from the same tone as your heart. When you are nervous, you become tense, which constricts the diaphragm, which in turn constricts your breathing, and your voice becomes high pitched, squeaky, fast and breathless. This takes you away from your heart sound, and so reduces the power and strength with which you speak.

- Relax your body
- Stand or sit comfortably
- Breathe deeply
- Speak slowly and clearly
- Avoid mumbling
- Avoid covering your mouth with your hand

Eye contact

Ideally, if you are speaking to a large audience, keep your head up, look towards the middle of the audience and from side to side. With a small group, make eye contact with individuals for a couple of seconds at a time.

- Avoid staring – this can be intimidating, and make people feel uncomfortable and embarrassed
- Avoid spending too much time looking at your notes or at a flipchart / PowerPoint screen. Have any notes in front of you, so that you don't have to turn away from your audience to look at them.
- Don't be distracted by people walking in or out or by something happening outside of the window – your students will follow your gaze

Answering questions

- Prepare answers to anticipated questions
- If you have a large audience, or a student who may be Deaf or have a hearing impairment, repeat questions and aim your reply to the whole audience
- When answering, and presenting generally, take your time; breathe before answering to allow you time to gather your thoughts

Maintain a positive attitude

Be positive! Before you speak, look at your students and tell yourself everything will run smoothly. Any negative thoughts or phrases that enter your head are likely to be your ego trying to help keep you safe (from its perspective). If they do enter, acknowledge they have done so for a reason and then let them go. Think positively and use positive affirmations. For example:

- I am happy to be here
- It is a joy and privilege to be here
- I am happy to see the students
- I am interested in the opinions and thoughts of my students
- We are about to share a profound journey *together* and they are on my side because they want to have a positive experience too

---

Teacher Tip – using an acupressure point to release anxiety

A very simple way of easing nerves is to apply gentle pressure to a particular meridian (energy) point, used by acupuncture and acupressure practitioners. It is used extensively in Emotional Freedom Techniques (EFT), and known as 'the karate chop point'.

Locate the part of your hand where you would do a 'karate chop'; on the outer side of your hand, half-way between the bottom of your little finger and your wrist. This point corresponds to the small intestine meridian, and is said to help alleviate feelings of doubt, increase feelings of confidence and self-esteem, and helps the memory.

Simply apply gentle pressure to this point and breathe deeply. It is worth trying this in the toilet or another quiet

---

place before you begin. You can even hold this point during your delivery, and it can look as if you are just holding your hands together. No one need know you are trying to calm any nervousness!

Don't worry if your students seem initially unresponsive. Most students are anxious about being asked to join in themselves. Remember, most people will admire anyone who gets up to speak in front of others. Watch other speakers/teachers, and pick out the positive points about the way they present.

Structure, preparation and channelling as a Spiritual Teacher

In many traditional management/presentation/training skills courses, it is taught that preparation accounts for 90% of the effectiveness of a successful session, with only 10% of the delivery being important to ensure success.

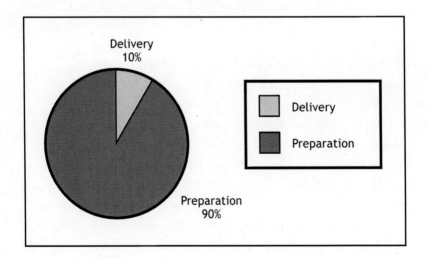

I do feel that this does not reflect what can often happen in spiritual teaching, where an element of openness to channelling (or inspiration) – whether it is obvious to students or not – may be needed.

What do we mean by 'channelling' in spiritual teaching?

As with many labels that we use, there are many different definitions of channelling.

Often channelling is perceived to be an obvious, overt communication where a person (e.g. a teacher) allows a 'higher being' or their 'higher self' to speak or write through them. Those who have witnessed a formal public channelling may have seen the channel enter into a trance-like state in which their tone of voice changed or their body movements altered; some people may have experienced seeing the face of the channel change or other visual signs that 'someone or something else' was present.

I would suggest that channelling is an experience of opening oneself to a greater wisdom and I feel that we can do this a lot as Spiritual Teachers. In fact, I believe that we all channel most (if not all) of the time, partly because we are all connected through our 'collective unconscious' as Jung described – or energetically as quantum physicists are now showing – and so we are all connected to some other wisdom all of the time. I do feel, however, that we are unaware of it because of the subtle nature of the information or communication – or inspiration – coming through.

Have you ever had the experience of a friend asking you for advice, where you gave the most profound, amazing, advice – and when your friend asked you to repeat it (so that they could write it down, for example), you couldn't remember what you said?

Or have you produced a report for a workplace, or an essay as a student, and – when you went back and read it some time later – you were amazed at what you had produced? (The 'Oh my

God, did I really write THAT?! How did I KNOW that?!' response.)

You may have witnessed someone giving you advice or communicating with you in this way, and felt that they had suddenly tapped into some amazing wisdom. To me, these are examples of everyday channelling, which I feel are significant to us as Spiritual Teachers.

For the purposes of this Handbook, when I talk about 'channelling', I am referring to the informal, subtle, everyday inspirational version, as described in the above examples – not the more formal 'standing-on-a-stage-and-bringing-through-a-being-of-light' version.

We can choose to be '90% prepared' for a session that we run; however, if we try to control the content of a session too much, we may find it difficult to allow ourselves to expand our delivery beyond the capabilities of the mind (ego). When teaching, we can allow ourselves to 'channel' just by creating space and time to allow a higher wisdom through. That wisdom may come to us using any of our senses; we may feel an answer, think of a response, or see some images, e.g. a significant memory, which can help us to respond to students. It helps to maintain a level of discernment, checking that what you are being guided to share is relevant and from your Higher Self.

Channelling versus Preparation – an example
I used to facilitate an evening development group called the London Starseeds Group at the London College of Spirituality. We used to travel in guided meditation to places in the galaxy or universe and connect with star energies. There was always an element of formal channelling by myself and/or others in the group.

Before the first few sessions, I would connect with my

---

guides, who would help me to prepare the content of the meditation, and the theme of the evening. Once I had become comfortable facilitating the group, my guides decided – as I was preparing for a session one evening – that they would not give me any guidance before the session. They made it clear that the entire evening was going to be channelled, including the meditation. I was going to have to just be open and allow my senses to guide me to everything I needed to communicate that evening.

As I am sure many of you can imagine, I had a quiet word with my guides. Then a few loud words. Then a meltdown. And they just laughed and told me I would be fine. Despite my anxieties, the evening was a complete success – not only that, I enjoyed the evening, once I had remembered to start breathing and just allow what needed to come through to come through!

I didn't tell the class what had happened until some weeks later – I didn't want them to pick up on my anxiety, and I wanted them to just enjoy the class without being concerned about me. But all of my Starseed group sessions were from then on facilitated with almost no formal preparation, and complete channelling – and I found that they were more powerful and inspiring as a result.

Of course with some workshops I facilitate, I spend much more time preparing and focusing on the structure. It depends upon the nature of course, the development needs of the students and the desired outcomes.

How can you know what to prepare and what to channel?
This will depend upon several factors, including:

- How comfortable you feel creating space for some or any

of your teaching to be channelled – especially in an informal way.

- The level of technical or knowledge-based learning that you are making available; knowledge-based learning tends to require more thinking and preparation on the part of the teacher – because you need to plan and prepare how you will present the information in a way that is easy for your students to remember. More experiential learning provides opportunities for more channelling.

- Any previous experience you may have of channelling, which will make you feel more comfortable in doing so.

Whatever you choose to do, feeling comfortable with what you are doing is the most important thing. You will of course have many experiences where your comfort levels are tested so that you can learn and develop as a teacher, but I do feel that this only ever happens when we are ready for the experience – and can deal with it! When you are ready to consciously open yourself up, you may find it a slightly nerve-wracking experience, but hopefully one that is rewarding and fulfilling.

Group Dynamics and Team Development

When a group of people come together to attend your course, or listen to you give a talk, you are bringing together a range of people from a wide variety of backgrounds, with different experiences, attitudes and expectations.

Wherever there is any audience participation or interaction, you will be providing those people with a platform to express themselves, to share a part of their experiences, beliefs and attitudes, and to help in the learning and development of everyone present. You will usually not be able to predict what someone might say or offer – especially if you have not met them previously. Yet you need to be aware of the impact that any one person has on another or on the group as a whole, as the contributions that any one individual makes can affect the learning experience of any number of other people in your group, by affecting the *dynamics* of the group. Dynamics are the relationships and interactions between people which affect how they develop together as a group.

The dynamics of a group are complex. It may be appropriate given the nature of your course for individuals to remain in their own space – particularly if the focus is on intensive self-development. Even in these situations, there are likely to be occasions where people are sharing something of their experience, and you would hope that the others in the group will be supportive of that. Also in these experiences, it is likely that there will be times where it would be helpful for everyone to *work together*. Getting group members to work together effectively – as a team – takes time. As the teacher, you need to be aware of your group's dynamics, and how these impact on the development of relationships within the group.

What is the difference between a group and a team? In a group, people behave as individuals. A group can develop into a team. A team is a group of people who work together towards a common purpose.

The process of changing and evolving dynamics could be termed as team development – in other words, how a group of strangers move towards working together as a team. The team's goals may simply be to grow and learn together for the duration of your course in a supportive, respectful way.

In 1965, Tuckman described four main stages which support the movement of group dynamics to that of a team; he added the last two stages in 1970. I first came across this theory as part of the work I did training student trainers with the National Union of Students.

The following information has been adapted from Tuckman's work to include the energetic and spiritual considerations of groups forming teams.

You may find that you experience these stages more obviously during longer, more interactive courses, or courses that take place over several weeks or months. You are less likely to experience these stages being overtly expressed during shorter courses.

1. **Forming**
2. **Storming**
3. **Norming**
4. **Performing**
5. **Mourning**
6. **Re-forming**

1. Forming

The key features of the forming stages are:

- The group is not yet a team, but rather a set of individuals.
- If you are running a longer course, there may be discussions where individuals define their purpose, roles and who they are.

- There may be a familiarity between seeming strangers based on soul connections. If two people feel an instant connection, it can impact on the rest of the experience for them and for others. They can be extra 'chummy' or 'cliquey', which might be wonderful for them, but might make others feel excluded. Or they might feel that the connection is one which needs healing, which can result in some uncomfortable feelings.

- The energy vibrations of each individual may already be changing as a result of connecting with others. They may be experiencing awakenings, rememberings, activations and healing consciously, subconsciously or unconsciously.

- Individuals who feel more sensitive to the energies of others may be more cautious – indeed this is very common when working in a spiritual teaching context. If a sensitive individual feels or believes that another person may be sapping them of their energies, or that the environment is not 'energetically clear', then they may avoid being near those people or fully relaxing in the learning environment.

- Transference may already be visible at this stage. This is where one person is reminded of someone they know in another context by someone else on the course. For example, Sue meets Jane. Jane reminds Sue of her mother, who she has had a difficult relationship with. Sue then behaves with Jane as she would with her own mother, rather than taking the time to get to know Jane for who she is. Of course, transference can operate in positive ways as well – some people may become very friendly with someone who reminds them of a person they like.

- At this stage, individuals tend to want to establish a personal identity within the group; to make some individual impression; on this basis, there may be a lot of ego-based expression.

2. Storming

Most groups then progress through a storming stage, during
  which:

- Some conflict is likely, as individuals and ideals are
  challenged.
- Personal agendas are revealed, with a degree of interpersonal hostility being inevitable.
- You might find that some people start to want to take on
  'roles' when working together with others – e.g. the
  carer/healer/leader etc, and this may come out during this
  stage because individuals are communicating who they
  are, and how they differ from other members of the group.
  These roles may reflect roles that they are comfortable
  playing in the outside world. Someone who is used to
  playing the role of healer/carer may need additional
  encouragement to focus on their development rather than
  the development of others during the course.
- Some individuals may be projecting their issues and
  insecurities onto others, based on unresolved relationship
  or other problems they may have in this lifetime.
- Individuals who are ungrounded may seek to become so
  by connecting energetically and unconsciously draining
  the energies of others, or may find it hard to move away as
  easily from being in their ego.
- Negative, as well as positive cords, may be forming (a
  reason why it is important to have created a safe space
  beforehand energetically).
- Karmic / soul contract / ancestral issues may be being
  played out here, possibly from another lifetime.
- Transference may continue to be present.
- Through skilful handling, new and more realistic objectives, approaches and norms can be established. Trust
  between group members can then start to develop.

3. Norming

The group/team now needs to establish norms and practices for itself:

- When and how should it work?
- How should decisions be taken (including intuitively)?
- What type of behaviour does it expect?
- What level of work and degree of openness, trust and confidence is appropriate? (Levels of trust will depend upon whether issues that have come up in previous stages have been worked through).
- At this stage, individual team members will be testing the temperature of the team, and measuring the appropriate level of commitment, and so discerning whether or not they can trust others.
- Individuals who may have felt that their energies were being affected by others – who they consider to be unbalanced or ungrounded – may have come back to a point of their own balance and of being in their own strength and power.

4. Performing

Only when the three previous stages have been successfully completed will the team be at full maturity, and able to be fully and sensibly productive and supportive.

- There may be a much greater energetic balance than there was previously, with a more even flow of energy between individuals – this may contribute to even greater trust.
- Working through the expression of the ego will often have been replaced by working through the Higher Self.

5. Mourning

At this stage, the team has finished its collective journey, and the members return as individuals to their previous lives.

- A degree of sadness may affect individuals as they part company with other members of the team – they may recognise this as being due to this situation or other situations in this or other lifetimes. There is a saying that 'in every goodbye, we have the ghost of every other goodbye'.[1]
- Significant healing may have taken place.
- It is important to close down energies, build energetic protection, and ensure that negative energetic connections have been broken
- Some individuals may not mourn for long, if they believe that their time together was for a perfect period of time.
- Individuals may stay in touch, but may not always recapture the intensity of the experience that they shared together during the course.

6. Re-forming

In some cases, teams may re-form to continue their learning, or to work together in some way.

- There may be comparisons between this re-forming and the previous experiences of the team. If the team do not capture the energy from the previous experience, individuals may feel demotivated, and the team may not work together as well. This is probable, as the re-forming is a completely new experience.
- Individuals will have grown and developed energetically as well as psychologically, and so may be surprised to meet people in a newer space.
- There may have been lots of experiences and developments that people will wish to share, and so more consideration may need to be given to managing time / allowing for more discussions and sharing.

- Care needs to be exercised, therefore, to ensure that exercises for re-forming teams are sufficiently different from previous ones, to prevent too many comparisons to the first experience.

Groups often need a leader to guide them, to help motivate and empower them. When a team is working well together, all they need is someone to facilitate and hold the space for them to continue to work on their collective goal. As a teacher, you will learn how to shape the dynamics of a group, and when it is appropriate to be a leader or a facilitator.

Group healing ... an exception to the rules?
Something unique happens when we connect with individuals for the purpose of a mass healing, or the anchoring of energies, or a mass meditation. In these situations, individuals are coming together to work as a team without having gone through the full team-development process. It may be that the collective working for a higher good may bypass the need to go through the same stages of development – including resolving the role of the ego. Or could it be that the energetic connections lead to personal and collective development in a way that takes us through the process unconsciously?

Games and Activities in Spiritual Teaching

As teachers, there are many ways in which we use activities and games that support the development of our learners, and that enhance the experience that they – and we – have.

There are several reasons why we use games and activities when teaching:

- To introduce people
- As icebreakers
- To divide the large group into smaller groups
- To energise the group
- To illustrate a concept
- To help switch students' attention
- To review learning
- To close a session

The appropriateness and the types of games and activities that we use can depend on a whole range of factors. These can include:

- The purpose of the games or activities – students are more likely to enjoy the games and to learn from them if the games are relevant to their learning, and they have a clear purpose.
- The appropriateness of the games – some exercises require close physical activity which may not be acceptable to some people for cultural or health or comfort reasons. Do allow students the choice of sitting out if they would like, or choose something more suited to those present.
- Health and safety – some games can be quite physical, so be aware of this. Do communicate the need to be careful with students if needed. Often more physical games can be

left out if there is a health and safety concern. This has meant that some 'fun' physical games are rarely if ever played now.

- The space available – check the size of the teaching environment before you carry out any activity.
- Having the materials that you need ready.
- The accessibility of some games – especially to disabled people, e.g. those with a physical or sensory impairment. You need to ensure that your activities are accessible to all (please refer to the chapter on Legislation). If one of your students tells you that they are disabled, find out of they need any reasonable adjustments to be made. You can discuss the course with them beforehand, which can include going through the exercises and how they are run, checking with them to find out if they need you to make any changes to them. You may need to choose different exercises in some cases.
- Allow for timings to change – some games and activities can take longer than anticipated, especially with larger groups who are having fun!

To introduce people

These games and activities help the group to learn about each other, and take place at the start of a course or workshop. Often people feel a little uncomfortable because they usually don't know others at this point in time, so asking people to open up too much can make them feel more uncomfortable, and so may take them longer to feel more at ease. Some students will also feel uncomfortable playing games that require a lot of activity in a room of people they don't know, e.g. ball throwing or dancing. This doesn't mean you can't use these games or activities – it just helps if you are aware of how they might feel if you do. If you do use something energetic, it does help to explain the purpose to everyone. Avoid asking any questions that are too revealing or personal at this stage.

Examples:

1. The heart-filled introduction

Prepare a flipchart showing a large heart divided into four chambers. Give each participant a piece of paper and ask them to draw a large heart in the middle of it.

Now invite participants to get to know each other by filling each chamber with information about the person they are sitting next to. If they know the participant, then ask them to sit with someone they don't know.

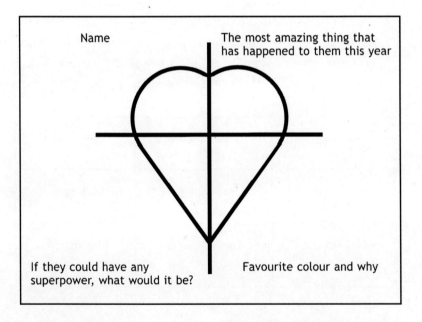

Ask each person to introduce their partner briefly to the group.

At the end, invite any participants who feel they can name all of the other members of the group to do so. Invite all students to do the same.

Variation in large groups: if you are working with a large

group where each person has a name badge, you can ask every student to put their badge in a pile in the middle of the room. Ask everyone to then pick out a name, find the person and work with that person in this or another exercise.

2. People bingo

With large groups: design a large 3 x 3, 4 x 4 or 5 x 5 grid on a page of A4 paper. Fill each box with a different characteristic (e.g. has blue eyes, is wearing a red item of clothing, looks happy, has travelled by train, lives in the North etc.). Give every student a copy of the 'Bingo Grid' and tell them that they need to find someone who fits every characteristic. They need to write that person's name in the relevant grid until they have a name in each box. The first one to complete their bingo grid and shout 'Bingo' wins! (You may even wish to give a prize! For example, a crystal / a pen / a toy.)

Has brown hair	Is wearing something red	Looks happy
Lives in the Northcrop	Has visited a circle	Can knit
Is wearing boots	Loves dancing	Has visited South America

3. Alliteration name game

Ask everyone to stand in a circle. As each person introduces themselves, ask them to say a sentence that includes a noun that starts with the same sound as their name, e.g. 'My name is Joe and I love to jog.' The next person in the circle must introduce all of the previous people (e.g. 'This is Joe and he loves to jog ...') before eventually getting to introduce themselves (e.g. 'My name is Dora and I like daisies').

4. Positive about me
Ask each person to write three positive statements about themselves on a post-it note and to then stick up the post-it note on a wall. Everyone has to guess who is who.

5. Alphabet descriptions
Ask each person to pick a letter of the alphabet, and then each person has one minute to describe themselves using only that letter.

6. Post-it greetings
Ask each person to take three post-it notes. On one, ask them to write a noun, on the second ask them to write an adjective, and on the third ask them to write a verb. Using their three words, invite each student to compose a greeting to the rest of the group.

Icebreakers
Icebreakers encourage people to leave their seats and interact with each other. They can help to reduce any resistances within the group to working together.

1. Hide and seek
Hide crystals / cards / koosh balls / other items and get the large group into teams to find them.

2. Tangle
Ask all students to stand in a circle. Ask them to hold out their hands in front of them and close their eyes. They then slowly step forward and try to find a hand to hold. Their left and right hands must hold one hand each, of different people. Then when they are ready, ask them to open their eyes. The

group must work together to unravel themselves without letting go of hands. When fully unravelled, they will be able to form a perfect circle.

3. Happy hugging

When giving out name badges or stickers at the start of a course, also give out a badge/sticker that says 'hug giver' or 'hug receiver' to each person. Ask everyone to stand up and on the command 'go', all the hug givers need to give all of the hug receivers a hug in as short a time as possible.

To divide the large group into smaller groups

1. Cards / crystals / toys / sweets and snacks

Put as many objects as you have people into your hand / a vessel and ask each student to pick one that allocates them to a particular group. For example, if you have eight people and need to divide them into two groups, you can use:

- 4 angel cards and 4 Ascended Master cards; or
- 4 clear crystals and 4 green crystals; or
- 4 tangle toys and 4 koosh balls; or
- 4 pistachios and 4 cashew nuts; or
- 4 red pens and 4 blue pens; or
- 4 crystals and 4 toys.

2. Self-sorting lines

Ask all the students to stand in line and order themselves according to a particular characteristic, for example:

- Date of birth
- Shoe size
- Star sign
- Height

- Alphabetical order of first name / surname / colour of top

Let the students know which end is which; for example, if asking people to arrange themselves in alphabetical order, let them know where 'a' is and where 'z' is. Once the students have arranged themselves in order, you can divide the line into as many smaller groups as you need (e.g. if you need two groups, then divide them into two by dividing in the middle of the line).

To energise

1. Flowering Random Acts of Kindness (RAOK)
Give every person a piece of square coloured paper, and ask them to write a RAOK that they have done for someone else on the paper. When they have finished, ask them to make an origami flower with it (you will have to demonstrate!), and then place it into the centre of the room. Ask everyone to pick a random flower and to read the RAOK – and once the lovely person has been identified, all celebrate the lovely RAOK! Instructions for easy origami lotus:
http://www.origami-instructions.com/origami-lotus.html

2. Loving life
Ask everyone to throw a ball/koosh ball/beanbag around the room. The person who receives the ball has to say what they love about life at that moment.

Variations can include: what you think about the sky / the summer / your favourite film / words associated with love or holidays or children etc.

3. Balloons
Divide the large group into two teams and ask them to play a relay exercise where they have to pick up a balloon using

chopsticks and take it to the other side of the room and back again without dropping it. The first team to complete the race wins.

Variations: relay races using fruit and spoons are an alternative. Everyone can then eat the fruit (if it hasn't been dropped!) to help raise energy levels as a snack.

4. Dancing

This is useful especially where energies need to be lifted. Using music that encourages dancing (e.g. dance music) is more effective than slower music; however, the type of music you choose can influence the nature and style of the dance, e.g. moving from a fast dance to a slow meditative dance.

5. Sheep and cows

Ask the group to stand up and close their eyes. Tell them that from that point onwards, they will not be allowed to open their eyes until the end of the game. Explain that you will now come around them and touch some of them on the shoulder. Do exactly that, obviously touching the shoulder of around half the group. Designate those who have been touched as sheep, and those who have not been touched as cows. Now ask everyone to only communicate using the sound of sheep (if they have been touched on the shoulder and designated sheep) or cows (everyone else). Invite everyone to wander around, making the relevant noise, trying to find all of the others making the same noise. Once the two groups have found each other, invite everyone to open their eyes and give a huge round of applause.

This can also be used to divide the large group into smaller groups.

Variations: cats and dogs / ducks and pigeons etc.

6. Never-ending sit-down

This game requires a medium to large number of participants.

Ask the group to stand in a circle – it is important that the circle is as accurate as possible. Then tell everyone to turn 90 degrees to their left. Now get everyone to side-shuffle towards the centre so that the circle gets smaller and smaller and people get closer and closer together. Again it is important that you keep the circle as close as possible to a real circle. When the circle is as tight and perfectly round as it can be, tell everyone that you are going to ask them to sit down on the knee of the person behind them. As long as everyone sits down together, it should work. If the circle sits down comfortably, try to get everyone to wave their arms. If they can do that, then you can try asking everyone to check that they are sitting on each other's right knee, and then put their left leg out and wave it about gently.

7. Sleeping lions

Ask the students to lie down on the floor, facing upwards with their eyes open. Tell the students that no one can touch anyone else during this game. You then have to try to make the students laugh or smile. If anyone laughs or smiles, then they have to stand up and help you make the other students laugh.

To illustrate a concept

These games and activities are used to encourage students to consider the issues that you are covering in your teaching.

1. Emotions and balancing

This activity invites students to consider the emotions that we experience, and how we respond to them. It is used in a range of personal development exercises – and is similar to a technique called the Rainbow Bridge in an energy-healing system called Emotrance.

Brainstorm a list of emotions that we feel towards other people regularly – write these up on the flipchart (e.g. excitement, joy, pity, anger, love, superiority etc.). Invite the students to choose one emotion on the list that they experience reasonably frequently regarding another person – an emotion that they would like to feel less –and invite them to visualise how they are with this person. Then ask them to visualise themselves with this person whilst feeling the opposite emotion. Now invite the students to imagine sending loving energy from the image of their usual experience with the person to the image that is loving, and back again. They might find that the more loving image increases in size, or comes closer. Allow the students to discuss how they feel following the exercise. Discuss how it is important to also accept ourselves for having these emotions towards others, and not judge ourselves – that can get in the way of healing the situation.

2. Self-disclosure

This is another exercise that is useful for illustrating how difficult we can find it to share all of ourselves with each other, and what happens with the emotions that we hold back.

Invite all of the students to write down three issues/secrets in their lives that they are NOT prepared to share with the rest of the group. Whatever is written must be written in private, and not shown to the others. You may wish to state that you will not – at any point – be asking anyone to share anything that they are writing down.

Explain and demonstrate that you are also taking part in this exercise.

Once everyone has written three issues down, lead a discussion with the group, bringing in the following points:

- how people feel having their issues there written down on a piece of paper (they are likely to feel very uncomfortable)
- why we have 'secrets'
- the importance of being able to reveal some of our personal issues to someone that we trust
- the difficulties of revealing these deep parts of ourselves to another person and what stops us from doing so
- what would help make it easier for people to be able to self-disclose
- self-disclosure, when it happens appropriately, can be a sign of us being aware of what we need to heal and reflect upon
- the more open we are about all of ourselves (again in an appropriate way), the more likely we are to be comfortable with the whole of ourselves, and be integrating all aspects of ourselves
- we do all have secrets, however, but it is important that we look after ourselves and that we avoid bottling up emotions and how we feel

To help switch students' attention

It is often helpful to conclude a session and move on to a new aspect by using a game to help to switch students' attention. As well as refreshing their minds, you can use it as an opening into the next session if you use something relevant to what you will next be learning about.

1. Brainteaser

Write the following words and number on the flipchart (ensure that these words are not visible to the students): Denmark, Elephant, Grey and 4. Now ask your students to do the following:

'Think of a number between 2 and 9. Multiply that number by 9. Add the 2 numbers together. Subtract 5. Now translate your answer into a letter, e.g. A = 1, B = 2, C = 3 etc. Now write the name of a country beginning with that letter. Next, write down the name of an animal beginning with the 2nd letter of the country you have written. Then write down the colour of the animal and how many legs it has.'

Then ask everyone to share their answers!

2. Name that tune

Divide the large group into two teams. Ask each team to take it in turns to sing a song to the other team, who have to guess the artist and name of the song. You can turn it into a competition with scores out of three or five songs each.

3. On being happy ...

On the flipchart, write the following phrases:

I'm happy when ...
I'm passionate when ...
I'm excited when ...
I'm relaxed when ...
I feel special when ...

Invite students to discuss this in pairs verbally or as a large group briefly.

To review learning

1. A to Z game

Write all of the letters of the alphabet on the flipchart. Point to each letter, one at a time, and invite students to state something that they have learned beginning with that letter.

2. Shark-infested waters

I used to use this when working with the NUS – it was always fun.

Put down as many pieces of paper on the floor as there are students, spread out. Describe how, in this game, those pieces of paper represent islands, sitting in a wonderful deep blue sea. Except the sea has sharks in it! Explain that you will be playing some music and that as long as the music is playing, they are safe from the sharks, but as the music stops, the sharks are coming up for some food so everyone needs to get to an island for safety. There will always be one less island than students playing, so one person won't be able to get to an island (like in musical chairs) – in this case, they can be saved by describing something that they have learned during the course or workshop. Once they have described something, they can sit down. Continue this process, taking away an 'island' every time the music stops, so that there is always one less island than people. Keep playing until the last person has given their answer. To create a safer environment, you can stick the paper down with blu-tack or masking tape (on hard floors). You can use masking tape on carpet.

3. Musical chairs

As above, you can use this game for reviewing purposes, by asking people to state something that they have learned when they haven't got to a chair.

To close a session

1. Thanksgiving circle

Ask all of the students to stand together in a circle, holding hands. Invite them to do any of the following:

- Give thanks for the learning by sharing one thing that they have enjoyed learning about
- State one new thing they will do in their lives as a result of

the course

- Chant using the 'Ohm' mantra or other similar sounds – this can be a very powerful way of closing off a session

Meditations in Spiritual Teaching

What is meditation?

There is often an assumption in spiritual teaching that meditation has to involve sitting in the lotus position in complete calm, silence and tranquillity. This is certainly one way to meditate; however, meditation itself is a term that encompasses a much wider definition.

For example, Madonna Gauding (2005) states that 'Meditation is simply making a choice to focus your mind on something. In fact, reading a book is a form of meditation, as is watching a movie ... focusing carefully on which bunch of bananas to buy is a form of meditation.'

Meditation does not require people to be seated in a quiet space. For the purposes of this chapter, I am referring to the types of meditations that are often used in spiritual teaching; meditations where people are having an individual personal experience enabling them to 'just be in the moment'.

You can use meditations in different ways to enable your students to have personal experiences and to connect with themselves and their journey. There are two types of facilitated meditations:

- Individual meditations where the students have a personal journey using music or silence
- Guided meditations, usually facilitated by the teachers

Individual meditations

These are a powerful way of enabling individuals to connect with their own inner peace, guidance and inspiration without any influence from you, other than as someone who is holding the space. It encourages individuals to have whatever experiences that they need at that time, due to the experience being almost completely non-directed.

It is often easier for individuals who have some experience and understanding of meditating in this way – some people find it very difficult to sit with themselves in a place of stillness, and so this can take a lot of practice before individuals feel truly comfortable with it.

Individual meditations can be practised in different ways. These are some suggestions; however, this list is not exhaustive:

- Focusing on a still, central point within the core of the body (often the navel, but it can be the heart or any other point), breathing into this point and releasing all thoughts.
- Allowing all thoughts to flow through the mind and then out.
- Quietly focusing on an external object such as the flame of a lit candle.
- Counting from 1 to 10 slowly, and as soon as a thought enters the mind, returning to 1 and counting from there again. The aim is to get to 10 without pausing (this can take a long time of practising!)
- Being in a place of calm stillness, breathing deeply, whilst listening to meditative music.

Guided meditations

Guided meditations provide individuals and groups with an opportunity to have an experience that is partly or fully guided by a teacher. People can be invited to have any sort of experience that fits in with the design of your course. You could, for example, facilitate a guided meditation that invites students to:

- Relax the main muscles in their physical body
- Heal an emotional difficulty, leading to forgiveness of others and/or the self
- Cleanse and balance their chakras
- Meet their inner child (or inner children)

- Connect with their hearts, and the feeling of unconditional love towards self and others
- Connect with their energetic selves (for example, different layers of their aura)
- Connect with the energy of an internal light, such as a lit candle emanating from the heart
- Travel to beautiful landscapes, such as a favourite travel destination, a beach, a waterfall, or a mountain
- Meet with spirit guides, angels, or other beings that guide and support a person
- Travel to other worlds, including other planets and star systems
- Travel to magical or other lands such as Atlantis, Lemuria
- Meet magical beings such as unicorns, fairies, dolphins or whales.

You can pre-prepare a meditation, or you can allow yourself to channel a meditation, being guided by what you feel or see or think or hear. Always choose what you are most comfortable doing, so that you can be as relaxed and your voice as soothing as possible for the benefit of those in the class.

Teacher Tips – facilitating a guided meditation
- If you are new to facilitating meditations, do practice beforehand.
- Inform students that their experiences will all be different – some people might see colours or images, others might have feelings or thoughts or hear sounds, some may not consciously have sensory experiences – and reassure students that whatever their experience, it is perfect for them at this time.
- Let students know that sometimes it is possible to

---

travel energetically in meditation, and that this is often an experience that is not consciously remembered (I have nicknamed this 'having a whiteout'). If this happens, this is fine and just an illustration of how far someone is travelling energetically.

- If there is a possibility that individuals might travel far energetically, or meet magical or otherworldly beings, ensure that you have cleared that space, and set your intention that all students will travel out and return safely. You can ask for additional protection if you would like for each member of the group, e.g. from Archangel Michael.

- Breathe slowly and gently yourself, to ensure that you are relaxed. It will also help to guide your students to breathe slowly and gently themselves.

- Speak slowly and connect with, and speak with, your heart sound.

- Allow pauses during the meditation so that individuals have the opportunity and time to have a personal experience.

- Always be clear about bringing every individual back into the present moment, so that they can connect with their physical bodies and be fully grounded into this reality. It is very important to ensure that this happens before students leave the room for lunch or at the end of the day. A hypnotherapy technique involves anchoring everyone using the same combination of words, so that whenever they hear those same words spoken, their subconscious mind recognises the commands that you are giving. For example: 'Now please bring your awareness back to this room, back to your physical bodies. Give your toes and fingers a wiggle, and when you are ready, open your eyes.'

The following is a guided meditation that supports the opening and balancing of the chakras. It includes the opening up and closing down of chakras at the end.

Opening and balancing the chakras: a meditation

Close your eyes and take a couple of deep breaths deep into your stomach. Breathe in peace. Breathe in love. Allow your breathing to become slower and deeper. Let go of all thoughts and release any tension from wherever you might feel it. Relax your shoulders and ensure that you feel completely comfortable and relaxed.

Begin by imagining yourself as a huge, old, wise oak tree, fully rooted to the Earth. Visualise thick roots coming out from underneath you, reaching through the layers of the Earth, reaching for the very core of the Earth. Allow Mother Gaia to hold those roots, anchoring you firmly to her.

Feel the Earth's energies flowing back up the roots and into your root chakra, allowing it to open into a beautiful ball of whatever colour energy your root chakra is. Notice if it feels as though there is too much or too little energy flowing through it. Allow the energy of the Earth to balance the flow of energy in your root chakra.

Allow this energy from the core of the Earth to continue to flow up to your sacral chakra, allowing it to open into a beautiful ball of whatever colour energy your sacral chakra is. Notice if it feels as though there is too much or too little energy flowing through it. Again allow the energy of the Earth to balance the flow of energy in your sacral chakra. Feel any excess energy flowing back down the roots into the core of the Earth.

Feel the Earth's energy flow up into your solar plexus chakra, allowing it to open into a beautiful ball of whatever colour energy your solar plexus chakra is. How does this chakra feel? Is there too much or too little energy flowing through here? Again, allow the energy of the Earth to bring the flow of energy in your solar plexus to a perfect point of balance. Allow all excess energy to flow back down to the core of the Earth.

Feel the Earth's energy flow further up into your heart chakra, allowing it to open into a beautiful ball of whatever colour energy your heart chakra is. How does this chakra feel? Is there too much or too little energy flowing through here? Again, allow the energy of the Earth to bring the flow of energy in your heart chakra to a perfect point of balance. Allow all excess energy to flow back down to the core of the Earth.

Feel the Earth's energy flow further up into your higher heart chakra, between your heart and your throat, allowing it to open into a beautiful ball of whatever colour energy your higher heart chakra is. How does this chakra feel? Is there too much or too little energy flowing through here? Again, allow the energy of the Earth to bring the flow of energy in your higher heart chakra to a perfect point of balance. Allow all excess energy to flow back down to the core of the Earth.

Now feel the Earth's energy flow further up into your throat chakra, allowing it to open into a beautiful ball of whatever colour energy your throat chakra is. How does this chakra feel? Is there too much or too little energy flowing through here? Again, allow the energy of the Earth to bring the flow of energy in your throat chakra to a perfect point of balance. Allow all excess energy to flow back down to the core of the Earth.

Allow the Earth's energy to travel further up again into your third eye chakra, allowing it to open into a beautiful ball of whatever colour energy your third eye chakra is. How does this chakra feel? Is there too much or too little energy flowing through here? Again, allow the energy of the Earth to bring the flow of energy in your third eye chakra to a perfect point of balance. Allow all excess energy to flow back down to the core of the Earth.

Now feel the Earth's energy flow further up once more up into your crown chakra, allowing it to open into a beautiful ball of whatever colour energy your crown chakra is. How does this chakra feel? Is there too much or too little energy flowing through here? Again, allow the energy of the Earth to bring the flow of energy in your crown chakra to a perfect point of balance. Allow all excess energy to flow back down to the core of the Earth.

Allow yourself to feel the flow of energy through your balanced chakras.

Allow all of the energy flowing from the core of the Earth through you to come through you and out of your crown. Visualise the pillar of white light coming out of your crown and going up and up and up, reaching for the core of the Galaxy. Notice how anchored you feel between the core of the Earth and the centre of the Galaxy. Allow the energies to flow between the Earth and the Galaxy through you.

Ending the meditation

We will now draw your energies back into you. Bring your attention to the energy flowing our through your crown chakra. Allow it to be released from the core of the Galaxy and to flow all the way back into you. Notice the beautiful ball of flowing energy at your crown. Release any excess energy and then allow your crown chakra to draw in completely around you. Now move down to your third eye chakra. Release any excess energy and then allow your third eye chakra to draw in completely around you. Draw the energy further down to your throat chakra. Release any excess energy and then allow your throat chakra to draw in completely around you. Notice the beautiful ball of flowing energy at your higher heart. Release any excess energy and then allow your higher heart chakra to draw in completely around you. Now move down to your heart chakra. Release any excess energy and then allow your heart chakra to draw in completely around you.. Draw the energy further down to your solar plexus chakra. Release any excess energy and then allow your solar plexus chakra to draw in completely around you. Now move down to your sacral chakra. Release any excess energy and then allow your sacral chakra to draw in completely around you. We will leave the red root chakra open. Feel all of these energies being drawn back down the roots extending from the soles of your feet, back down into the core of Mother Earth.

Imagine yourself being placed in a wonderful thick cloak of protection, made of all of the crystal, colour and geometric energies that you need for your healing, protection and grounding at this time. Zip up the cloak, pull the large hood over your head, put a lovely warm scarf on and some lovely thick gloves and put a nice thick pair of boots on. Place yourself in a golden dome of protection. Finally, check that you are fully grounded by connecting with yourself , as the old wise oak tree that you visualised being at the start of this journey. Notice the very thick roots coming out from underneath you, anchoring you to the core of the Earth.

When you are ready, please bring your awareness back to this room, back to your physical bodies. Give your toes and fingers a wiggle, and when you are ready, open your eyes.

Discussion topic – closing down chakras
Traditionally, teachers use a closing meditation that closes down the chakras before students leave a development class. The reason for this is to ensure that students' energies are closely drawn around them, keeping them protected.

More recently, there has been some debate around this, as some teachers and students feel that this will impede the natural and healthy flow of energy through the chakras. A clear illustration of this is the concept of closing down the heart chakra – I am often asked 'Doesn't this stop love flowing through?'

As with all aspects of your teaching, you need to discern what feels appropriate to you. I would suggest, however, that it is not be necessary to close down the chakras per se; but that it is important to ensure that students are fully grounded and protected before leaving any class. This does not necessarily need to include closing down the chakras, but it can include encouraging students to draw their energies around themselves, sealing or protecting their energies and becoming fully present and connected with their physical bodies. I still, however, choose to close the chakras, for the benefit of students who feel more grounded and protected when they have closed their chakras down; it is important to me that my students leave feeling safe and grounded!

Grounding and Protection

Grounding

Grounding, protection and energetic hygiene are areas that are commonly talked about by Spiritual Teachers, but when I was first stepping onto my spiritual path, I found them confusing.

I was often admonished by some people for being 'ungrounded', but I didn't know what I was doing wrong to be 'ungrounded', and at times I found it too difficult to ask what I should do – as though I might look stupid for not really understanding what people meant. The word 'grounding' is used with such commonality in spiritual contexts, that there is often an assumption that 'everyone knows what it is'. But I didn't, and have come across many able and gifted students who didn't either.

This is an example of how jargon can make learning opportunities inaccessible. It is always advisable not to make assumptions about individuals' knowledge, and to clarify even seemingly basic definitions like this for the benefit of all.

Avoid assuming that students – particularly students who are new to you – have the same basic understanding of spiritual concepts that you do. I would always advocate ensuring that everyone – no matter how advanced – understands the same basics before you move on together with your learning.

So, what is being grounded? *It is literally being connected or rooted to the present time and present moment.* Therefore, being ungrounded is a state of not being connected to the present moment.

Being grounded is important for several reasons:

- It helps to ensure that we are present enough to learn what we need or choose to.

- It means that we can connect with other people, listen and communicate with them effectively.
- We can make decisions based on what feels right at the time, rather than based on past or future fears.
- All healing and protection needs to be anchored into our whole physical and energetic being. We need to be grounded for that anchoring to take place effectively.
- It is necessary in order to receive clear Divine communication or to connect with our Higher Self and bring through clear guidance and wisdom.
- It makes it easier for us to connect with our own strength, power and personal truth.

How can you tell if someone is ungrounded? The following are possible signs:

- They are not listening
- They ask lots of questions
- They are very fidgety – not relaxed (e.g. leg twitching)
- They are distracted – they may do things like putting tissues in the fridge, or orange juice on cereal instead of milk
- They find it difficult to connect with earthly activities easily
- They laugh a lot for no apparent reason – sometimes this can be nervous laughter
- They forget easily
- They find it difficult to get anything done – having lots of ideas, but finding it difficult to follow through
- They are flustered
- They find it hard to make decisions
- They are talking to spirit all of, or a lot of, the time – not really connecting with their earthly lives
- They seem agitated

- They get easily frustrated.

Some simple techniques for improving grounding

You may have your own methods that you enjoy using. Here are some additional suggestions:

- When meditating, always sit with both feet or your body connected to the floor. You can imagine thick roots coming out of the bottoms of your feet, or from underneath your body, and going through the layers of the Earth and anchoring you into the core of the planet.
- You can visualise yourself as a rabbit, digging into a burrow under the Earth, being completely surrounded by soil.
- You can visualise Lady Gaia reaching up from the core of the Earth and pulling you down into it.
- Some people hold or connect with crystal energies such as black tourmaline, hematite, bloodstone, garnet and pyrite. Copper is a useful grounding metal as it is a natural conductor.
- You can touch any plant or tree, whether it is an indoor plant or a tree in a park. Walking barefoot on grass, soil or sand is very grounding too.
- Moving, walking and especially dancing are very helpful for many people; the more vigorous you are, the better.
- Wearing the colour red or visualising the colour red around you is very helpful. Red is a colour associated with grounding.
- For those who like to connect with the Angelic Realms, you can call on your guardian angels to help you to ground, or Archangel Sandalphon. His energy frequency is said to be the same as the colour red.
- Drinking water and eating food – particularly protein – can be very helpful.

- Some people find drinking coffee to be grounding, as it brings them into the present and can help with focus. Other people find that coffee has the opposite effect, and makes them feel completely ungrounded!
- You can check by asking your Higher Self how grounded you are from 0 to 100 percent. Notice the first answer that you get, and accept it. If you are not 100% grounded, you can choose to do something about it. You may find it helpful to practise doing this several times a day.
- Telling yourself to ground by saying 'Ground, ground, ground …' repeatedly until you feel grounded.
- Saying 'I am 100% fully grounded in this moment, in this reality' three times.

Is being grounded just an energetic process?

Some people find that it doesn't matter how much visualisation work they do to ensure that they are grounded, they do not feel that they are grounded. I think that this is common in situations where there are emotional reasons for someone being ungrounded.

For example, some people find it difficult to connect with being in the present moment because they are emotionally or mentally connecting with past hurts or future anxieties. And so being ungrounded can be very common in people who are experiencing emotional or mental difficulties.

In these cases, working energetically to ground may not be enough. Other grounding support may be needed, including talking through problems or anxieties with a friend, counselling or other similar therapeutic interventions. It is amazing how grounding a good emotional release – for example, a good cry – can be!

Protection

Energetic protection can be a difficult and challenging concept for many people – teachers and students alike – for it often brings up issues that can make people feel fearful. In my experience, it is an important area to address when it does come up in a workshop – as it is often a question that is present in the 'backs of people's minds' in some way.

Not everyone is comfortable with the word 'protection' because it can support the concept of being 'separated' from each other, as though we should remain separated. When we come from a place of love, it could be said that we do not need to separate from (or protect ourselves from) others – indeed that our spiritual journeys are about us integrating and coming to a place of Oneness with everything and everyone.

The first thing I would suggest here is that you again check what resonates with you. In my own personal experience, I feel that needing to ensure that we are protected *and* coming to a place of Oneness are both relevant and can co-exist at the same time. For example, it may be that learning to heal ourselves and be in our full strength and power leads us to being fully protected all of the time. However, based on my own experiences, I do feel that many of us do not *begin* our lives/journeys in our full strength and power and are in need of healing, and that lower frequency energies can connect with any 'chinks in our armour'.– weak spots in our energetic selves. Also, even when we connect with our own strength and power, it is a challenge to always remain in this state.

Can't I just ignore this aspect of spiritual teaching if it doesn't resonate with me?

People can be afraid of the 'unknown' (e.g. so-called 'dark' or 'lower frequency' energies), so if the question of protection is raised in a group, I would suggest that it needs to be addressed –

even if it is something that doesn't resonate with you personally. If you ignore this as an issue once it has been raised, some people will perhaps partly feel better because they haven't had to consider this subject area, but even they will be left feeling uncomfortable. The energy of the group is likely to fall rapidly as fear sets in, so the most empowering way of dealing with the situation is to address it positively and raise energies. By addressing it positively, you can allay students' fears, which will allow them to return to feeling that they are in a safe environment. Leaving students in a state of discomfort or even fear will interfere with their ability to learn, and it may change their perception of the whole learning experience. Also, it may be that another student may benefit from understanding more about this subject area.

You, as a tutor, may not have had personal experience of lower frequency energies – it is OK to state this to students. However, this does not mean that others do not have these experiences, and it is one area for us Spiritual Teachers where it may be more responsible to respect that others may have had these experiences, and to acknowledge the existence of shadow rather than to ignore it – whatever your own experiences may have taught you. So it may be helpful to discuss what different perspectives are from a place that is loving, safe and respectful of those who may feel this resonates with them. If your own experiences don't enable you to further support your students in this area, then do signpost them to other sources of information.

For more on all of this, I would thoroughly recommend Sue Allen's *Handbook on Spirit Release* (please see the Further Reading section at the back of this book).

What are we seeking to protect ourselves from?

Your perceptions and your students' perceptions of what you might consider protecting yourself from will vary, but can include:

- The energies of others, which might be out of balance and/or in need. It is quite usual for students, for example, to 'look up to' their teachers, and feel as though they need something from them. This can lead to some students energetically seeking some of the teacher's energy – usually completely unintentionally. This can often happen when student s and teachers don't feel themselves to be equals in the learning journey.

- Earthbound spirits – these can come in many forms. There are many different beings in the spirit realms that have not left the earthly dimensions, for many different reasons, or could leave but choose to stay because they have a purpose in doing so. Usually they have not felt ready to move away from the Earth – from family members or friends that they love, or people they might be upset with. They might not understand that they have left the Earth and passed into spirit. Some might have a contract with a person on the Earth to fulfil. Some of these spirits are benevolent, some can be malevolent. Even the malevolent spirits have their own fears and need compassion, and need to feel loved – as we all do when we are in a place of fear.

Below is a suggested explanation that you could use with students to help them to feel safer, whilst acknowledging their feelings. It is important when discussing this with students that you do so calmly, confidently, assertively, lovingly and positively. Your students will feel any anxieties you have, so it is important that you deal with these yourself beforehand.

Make sure that you stand up as you talk, and gently move *towards* the group (do not sit down or move back when discussing this – by standing, you lift your energies, and help to change the energies of the group before you have even started talking):

'We are all said to be made up of a Light side, and a shadow side. It is said that our journey to "enlightenment" involves integrating these two dualistic aspects and becoming whole and One – and in so doing, experiencing Oneness with everyone and everything. So until we reach that point of total integration and Oneness, we are working with both our Light and our shadow in some way. Even if we focus on working with the Light part of ourselves, we still cannot ignore the shadow. Part of our learning and development involves learning about our shadow, understanding our shadow from a place of compassion and wisdom, and then we can give those shadow parts of ourselves the opportunity to heal and integrate through that understanding.

'In the same way that there are those of us who are connecting more with the Light part of ourselves on the Earth, there are also those who are connecting more with the shadow part of themselves. We all meet people we would probably try to avoid in some circumstances, because we feel that they are connecting more with the shadow parts of themselves. They will be doing so for a large number of reasons, usually because it is where they are choosing to be for now. Their soul may be growing through the experience. There could also be all sorts of other factors such as karma playing out through them and their relationships.

'When we pass into spirit, we can continue to connect with the Light or shadow part of ourselves in exactly the same way – just because we have gone to 'another place' doesn't mean that we are ready to let go of what mattered to us when we were on the Earth.

'So in spirit, the same thing is being played out. Some would say that there *are* beings that are working from a place of shadow energetically, but they are just in their journey, exploring that part of themselves, as we all do at some point. The best that we can do is show compassion and love, and support any being – like any person – who is working from a place of shadow to be reminded of the Light within themselves.

'Whenever we come across a situation involving a being that

is connecting more with their shadow (meaning that they are vibrating at a lower frequency energy), the best we can do is to stay strong and compassionate and call in love and Light to help enable them to find their way home to the Light, if that is what they need help with and are ready to choose. They may not be ready to do this, and that is their choice – all we can do is provide an opportunity for healing, and stay strong. Ultimately, it is a situation that can support your learning and growth too. Protection is just about completely believing in your own strength and power and not allowing yourself to be affected by any low-frequency energies in any form. You can also call on beings of Light to help you clear your energies and to stay protected, if you believe in them.'

Methods of protection

This you can do with your intent. I would recommend checking that you feel protected on a regular basis – some teachers recommend every morning, evening and every time you go to a place where lots of people are gathered, whether that be an event or travelling on public transport.

Different people use different ways of protection and you will find what works best for you. Here are some examples that you may use already, or might like to try:

- Ask your guides and protectors, that are working for 100% Light *only*, to place you in a gigantic pillar of Light, within a completely sealed Golden Dome of Protection around you. State aloud that you only invite beings working with 100% pure Light and Love to be present at all times, and ask your guides to keep you safe and protected.
- For those who like to connect with the Angelic Realm, Archangel Michael is a being of Light who uses his energies to protect. You can also ask Archangel Michael, after meditating, to ensure that all doorways and gateways

that you may energetically travel through are completely closed when you return to the Earth.

- You can visualise yourself in a platinum suit, or a platinum cloak imbued with all of the colour, crystal and geometric energies that you need for your healing and protection at that time.
- For those who like to connect with Archangel Michael, you can visualise yourself in his blue cloak of protection.
- You can imagine yourself in a lead suit.
- You can consciously draw your energies in closer to you.
- You can imagine being in a giant mirrored disco ball, keeping all of your energies for you, reflecting away anything that isn't working for 100% pure Light and Love only. You can fill the giant disco ball with a range of colours, such as red for grounding and white or blue for protection.
- When you are in the company of others, you can – with the permission of their Higher Self – help to raise their energies and protect yourself further by sending them the Gold and Silver Violet Flame (see under 'Energetic cleansing' below) or sending them a shower of love and happiness.
- You can ask that your Merkabah,[2] or aura, which I understand to be a crystalline grid structure, be infused with the energies of platinum, and then completely sealed in the energies of gold. It is also helpful to ensure that one's aura is completely sealed in golden light before doing significant energetic healing work.
- State 'I am 100% protected from all lower-frequency energies through all time and in every reality' three times.
- *Ask for LOVE as well as Light.*

The strongest means of ensuring our own protection is through healing what we can and coming to a place of our own strength and power. This means healing physically, emotionally, mentally and spiritually.

If you encounter a being and you are unsure of who they are or why they have visited, feel free to ask them 'Are you working for 100% pure Light and Love only?' There is said to be a Universal Law of Challenge which states that you can ask this three times and all beings have to state the Truth if challenged on the third go. So, if on the third go, they say 'no', simply ask them to leave and welcome in your guides and protectors who are working for 100% pure Light and Love only.

Energetic cleansing

However protected we feel we are, there may perhaps be times when we don't feel as energetically clear as we would like. We might feel confused, be thinking about the same situation or person again and again, or feel unable to move on in some way. Using any of a range of cleansing processes can help us to come our own sense of balance and strength more easily.

These can include:

- Visualising all lower-frequency energies flushing out from you when you have a shower, and down the plug hole – and turning into lovely clear cleansed beautiful water as it does so
- Having a cold shower, to help give your body and aura a bit of a 'wake-up', which can be very cleansing and releasing
- Visualising yourself sitting within the Gold and Silver Violet Flame; this is a flame that is said to transmute – literally change – lower-frequency energies into the highest-vibrational energies
- Cord cutting (see below)
- Dagger lifting (see below)
- Cutting karmic ties (see below)

Cord cutting

In every interaction that we have with people, animals, situations and places, there is an exchange of energy. Where those interactions are balanced and loving, energy flows freely through 'positive'3 cords. When those interactions take place where there is an imbalance, or if we or others feel needy in any way, then 'negative' etheric cords are created that connect us with that person or situation. Cords are a bit like energetic rubber tubes. Cords can lead to an unbalanced exchange of energy if the other person or situation needs some of our energies, or we can drain energy from other people or situations. Cords can exist across lifetimes as well as through this one.

Whenever a person feels in less than a whole or loving state, it may be that cords are involved. When a person finds it difficult to stop thinking about a situation or person, there may also be cords involved.

You are likely to have your own sword, or other tools, to cut through etheric (energetic) cords so that there is no longer an unbalanced transfer of energy. These tools can include using a laser, or a large cutting machine – any means by which you can comfortably cut through the cords. For those that connect with the Angelic Realm, Archangel Michael has a beautiful platinum and sapphire sword that he can use.

Some cords can be very tough to cut through, especially if they have existed for a long time. It is also important to be completely clear in your intention to have the cords cut – otherwise you may not be successful on your first attempt.

The following meditation can be used to connect with your own cord-cutting tools, or to call in Archangel Michael to cut any negative cords.

1. Begin by closing your eyes, and take a few deep breaths into your stomach. Connect with that sense of peace and

balance and release all tension wherever you may feel it in your body.

2. Bring your awareness to the situation or person with which you would now like healing to take place, or to the whole of your energy field. You can ask Archangel Michael to be with you. Feel his presence. You may see, hear, feel or just know that he is with you. He carries the energy frequency that corresponds with the colour blue, and you may sense this blue energy around you.

3. Using your inner voice, or speaking aloud, ask yourself or ask Archangel Michael to cut all negative cords connected to a situation, person, or all situations and people, across all time frames, realities or dimensions for the highest good of all concerned.

4. Visualise the ends of the cut cords being healed, and you and all those you have been connected to, being surrounded by love and light. You can also ask Archangel Raphael to help heal the cord ends.

5. If you have called on other beings, such as the angels, to help you, offer your thanks to them.

6. Bring your awareness back to the room.

Cords can re-form, so it is good practice to cut cords at least twice a day, in the morning and at night.

Dagger lifting

You can use this method on yourself or another. When people are angry at themselves or others, they send that anger energetically.

Those thought-forms can imbed inside the body or aura, for example in the form of a 'dagger'. This can happen when we curse ourselves or others unconsciously or consciously.

Ensure that you sit or lie comfortably, and relax. Breathe in peace and love. If you work with angels, you can also call upon Archangels Raphael and Michael to surround you and breathe in and out very deeply. Be willing to let go of and lift any anger energy from your body from wherever it is held, in all time frames, realities and dimensions. Release any daggers, arrows, swords, or other sharp or painful objects from your back or other areas. As these daggers and other objects now lift from your body, you may surprised to learn who sent them to you. Be willing to send those people your love and acceptance to the best of your ability as a way to heal yourself even further. Keep lifting the objects out of your entire body, letting go of them completely.

Allow yourself to be covered in a liquid green healing gel which immediately heals away any former incisions. As you heal, allow Michael to cover you in a shield of purple rubber which ensures that any further attacks will bounce away from you. Ask that, as they do so, they will be transmuted into love.

Thank Archangels Michael and Raphael for the healing, if they have been present.

You can also ask that all daggers that you may have sent to others (even if unintentionally) are removed in all time frames, realities and dimensions.

Karma and karmic ties

Karmic ties are energetic connections that we have to particular lessons, circumstances or situations that we have agreed to experience in order to facilitate our soul's growth, journey and evolvement.

The Universal Law of Karma works alongside the Universal Law of Harmony, in which we attain harmony and balance.

Whenever you act with intention, you create karma. The Law of Wisdom is the universal law that recognises that wisdom dissolves karma.[4]

Karmic ties can be made to people or situations, and may have been made across lifetimes, if harmony has not yet returned to a particular situation.

The Lords of Karma

The Lords of Karma – or Powers – are said to be angels that can help us to remove karmic ties, and to be more in our conscious full strength and power.

They are said to protect our souls and look after our Akashic records.[5] Because of their role as keepers of our Akashic records, they have the power to absolve karmic lessons, once we are ready for this to happen. Often, we need to be aware of the reason of why we have a particular karmic tie in order for it to be released, for we need to be consciously aware of what the lesson has been.

Karmic ties are said to be constantly made and unmade, and so some challenges may occur if, with our intent, we act in a way that is consciously disharmonious.

In order to ask for karmic ties to be cut, connect with and ask the Lords of Karma if the karmic ties can be released. You may be shown the reasons for the karma, and asked what you have learned in relation to the situation before the Lords of Karma decide whether or not a karmic tie is ready to be cut. Once a decision has been made for any karmic ties to be cut, they may be taken to the Void, a place of infinite possibilities and ultimate creation. The Void is said to be a place where permanent change can be effected, and so allowing the ties to be taken to the Void allows them to be permanently dissolved.

Energetically Cleansing
the Teaching Environment

There are many methods for energetically cleansing your environment. This is not an exhaustive list; you may have your own preferred means of doing so. The most important approach, as with all energy work, is setting a clear intention.

Methods of space clearing

- **Visualise and invoke a pillar of white or golden Light**
  You can, with your intention, create it to fill a room or a building, and to cleanse all people and beings that come within it of any lower-frequency energies.

- **Invoke a clearing vortex**
  Visualize a small whirlwind of crystalline white fire around you or within a workshop space – like an upside triangle. Allow it to flow like a whirlwind, and with your intention, allow it to transmute all lower-frequency energies, or to carry the energies down to Mother Earth to heal.

- **Call upon the Angelic Realms and ask them to clear the space**
  You can call on Archangel Michael to clear and cleanse a space – Archangel Michael serves on the first ray and his specific function is to provide protection. He can also surround you and your workshop space in a completely sealed golden dome of protection. Other Archangels and Ascended Masters that you can call on include Archangel Sandalphon, Archangel Metatron and Melchizedek.

- **Use the Platinum Net**
  Call on Melchizedek, the Mahatma and Metatron to bring down the platinum net through you, the people in your workshop, the room and the building. The Platinum Net is said to clear all lower-frequency energies.

- **Invoke the Gold and Silver Violet Flame**
  Call on St Germain, an Ascended Master who is keeper of the Gold and Silver Violet Flame, to use it to transmute all lower-frequency energies in a room or building.

- **Use a space-clearing invocation**
  An example of one is given at the end of this section.

- **Use Reiki symbols**
  With your intention, use Reiki symbols which you can imagine or physically draw into the space, to clear and cleanse it of all lower-frequency energies.

- **Use sound/toning**
  Crystal and singing bowls are helpful for use in clearing energies. Also, you may wish to tone (chant) the 'Ohm' at least three times, or your soul name – if you know it.

- **Use crystal-energised space-clearing sprays**

- **Use salt**
  Sprinkle salt over the floor areas, leave for a short while and then vacuum up. Of course, this is likely to only be practical to use in your own home.

Remember: intention is the most powerful and important aspect of space clearing. Be clear with your intention to clear a space, using any of these or other methods. You can send the clearing forward or back in time, and across all time, space and realities.

Opening your workshop / Clearing the space (Dr Joshua Stone)

This is one example of a space-clearing invocation. You can use this process to prepare your workshop space. You can read this at the beginning of a workshop as a meditation, or you can prepare the space before the delegates arrive.

Establishing the Ascension Column and Pillar of Light

'I call in the Planetary and Cosmic Spiritual Hierarchy to establish and activate a gigantic ascension column in the room. I ask that it be connected to a gigantic pillar of light and to this group's planetary and cosmic *antakarana*, the tube of light that connects us with our monad and God. I ask that the pillar of light contain the white flame of Ascension and that it be connected to the Ascension flame in the temple of Luxor.'

Clearing with the Platinum Net

'I call forth to Melchizedek, the Mahatma and Metatron to bring down the platinum net through the entire group, this room and this building. Platinum is the highest-frequency color available to Earth. The only higher frequency is the clear light of God, which has no colour. The platinum net will clear this group, this room and this building of all negative and imbalanced energies on all levels.'

As you become more confident with using the Platinum Net you may want to extend the clearing further to the town, country or even planet.

Axiatonal Alignment

'I now call again to the Planetary and Cosmic Hierarchy for a planetary and cosmic axiatonal alignment. This will balance all meridians of each individual and instantly align the group energy with God and the consciousness of the Spiritual Hierarchy on all levels.'

The Ascension Flame
'I now call to the Spiritual Hierarchy and inner-plane Ascended Masters to anchor and activate the golden white Ascension Flame. You will instantly feel and even see this energy coming in now.'

Invoking the Spiritual and Cosmic Hierarchy
'I now call to the entire Spiritual and Cosmic Hierarchy to join this workshop. I ask that the appropriate master step forward to overlight this workshop.'

If there are particular Masters you personally are connected with, this is the time to call them forward. If you want to you can also suggest that the individuals within the group call forth the Masters that they would like to assist in this workshop.

The Soul and Monad Mantras
The soul mantra was given by Ascended Master Djwhal Khul to the Earth through the channellings of Alice Bailey. It is one of the most profound mantras on the planet and should be recited every time any spiritual work is about to be ignited. The original soul mantra goes as follows:

I am the Soul,
I am the Light Divine,
I am Love,
I am Will,
I am Fixed Design.

I am the Monad,
I am the Light Divine,
I am Love,

I am Will,

I am Fixed Design.

Michael's Golden Dome of Protection

'I now call for Archangel Michael and his legion of angels to create a golden dome of protection for the group. Archangel Michael serves on the first ray, and his specific function is to provide protection.

'I also ask that each member of this group is protected by Archangel Michael and his legion of angels as we continue on our spiritual paths and in our work in service to the Light.'

Humility in Spiritual Teaching

Humility is a significant concept in spiritual teaching – but it can also be elusive. It means different things to different people. This chapter will offer some suggestions as to what humility is, and isn't. These suggestions are based on students' responses on the Spiritual Teacher's Development Course. As with everything else, please do check what resonates with you!

Being humble is ...

- being willing to accept that things may be other than the way you think they are
- being willing to serve others / be aware of others' needs
- the opposite of arrogant
- being genuinely interested in people because you want to learn from them
- being a more effective listener – because you want to grow and learn
- being transparent
- being able to comfortably state in public 'I don't know'
- being in a place of power
- being patient
- showing unacknowledged kindness
- being honest
- being thankful
- accepting others and situations as they are
- appreciating simple things
- respecting others
- being understanding
- being modest
- being charitable
- having unity consciousness

- being kind and gentle

Being humble isn't ...

- dishonouring others' opinions and experiences
- being unsympathetic
- disrespecting others
- coming from an exaggerated ego
- behaving arrogantly
- behaving inflexibly
- behaving domineeringly
- always talking about yourself
- working without integrity
- being judgemental
- making assumptions

Self-development questions

1. If you could score yourself on a scale of 0 to 10, 0 being not at all humble, and 10 being humble, how would you score yourself?
2. What do you feel the ideal score would be for you as a Spiritual Teacher and why? (You might feel that it is important for you to be humble to the score of 7, for example, rather than 10).
3. Is there is a difference in your ideal and actual score?
4. If so, what can you do to ensure that your ideal and actual scores are the same?
5. When teaching, what prevents you from being as humble as you would like to be, and what can you do to overcome these barriers?

The Ethics of Spiritual Teaching

Awareness and integrity are hugely important concepts in spiritual teaching. Ethics can be taken to be several things, including a set of principles, or a code of conduct that differentiates between what may or may not be helpful and indeed appropriate in any situation. The use of the word 'appropriate' can suggest some level of judgement, so here I am using it in the context of checking what resonates. Above all, ethics requires self-awareness and being conscious of oneself as a teacher, and we will explore some of the ethical questions that can arise in this chapter. This is not intended as a code of conduct that you need to follow; it simply raises questions that we all face, with some guidance that may be helpful.

Empowering, inspiring and enabling

As Spiritual Teachers, we are often trusted with some of the most important and profound aspects of a person's journey. People can come to us and choose to be our students for many reasons, all of which mean that we are in a position of leadership and responsibility. We need to be mindful of respecting other people on their journey, helping them to hold onto their own power. It is important for us not to take their power. Others may turn to us for answers, and we can share our learning and experiences. It may be most helpful to our students to ensure that they have opportunities to develop skills and experiences of their own, helping them to build their confidence. Empowering, inspiring and enabling others to understand their own abilities is more helpful to them and you than allowing them to build a dependency or attachment to you or your teachings. That way, we can help to draw out the best in everyone, including ourselves.

There is a popular proverb that beautifully summarises this idea: 'Give a man a fish, and you feed him for a day. Teach the man to fish, and you feed him for a lifetime.'[6]

Be conscious of your own journey

We all regularly come out of being in a place of balance. As Spiritual Teachers, it is helpful for us to recognise and acknowledge this for ourselves, so that we can choose to do something about it. In an ideal world, we might perhaps choose to be in a place of balance all of the time – especially before teaching. The reality of life and our own spiritual journey is such that we may arrive somewhere to facilitate a workshop or course and be out of balance; maybe the train was running late, or we encountered a difficult situation during our journey, or we are feeling nervous or anxious before the teaching. Maybe we are facing many challenges in our own lives. As was described earlier in the section on the 'Inspirational Spiritual Teacher', as long as you are consciously aware of how balanced you are emotionally, spiritually, physically and mentally, you can then make choices about how to ensure that this isn't projected onto your students, so they don't feel like they need to support you. This is where it helps us to leave our needs outside of the learning environment.

This is not about hiding anything or being dishonest. It is about respecting the space that students need to evolve and grow – their reason for coming to you. As we have already mentioned, it may be entirely helpful to share our own personal journeys – once we have resolved them ourselves first and so do not have an emotional reaction.

Integrity

None of us knows all the answers – most of us know very few; and even then, they are the answers that resonate with us. Being honest about what we don't know reflects integrity as well as humility. Knowing how and when to refer students to others is an important way for us to be in our integrity.

It is also important to aim to do ourselves what we advise others to do. If we are not always in balance, then can we ask our students to be the same? Are we in a position to admonish them if they are not (which I have encountered some teachers doing!)? We might portray ourselves as being permanently balanced to others, but this can make it more difficult for our students to connect with us as having the same 'real life' experiences that they do, if we do not communicate some aspect of how we are equal human beings with them.

Maintaining our own spiritual practice

This does not have to involve spending an hour in silent meditation every day. This can be a challenge when we are busy – just as much for us as it is for our students!

One of the difficulties that I had when meeting other Spiritual Teachers was that I always felt like a bit of a fraud because I don't do very much silent 'lotus position with hands in a mudra' meditation myself, and so I thought I was not 'as good as' other colleagues who teach.

At a wonderful workshop with William Bloom, we discussed how the purpose of any meditation is to help us to connect with that Divine 'wow' amazing joy / peace / love feeling. And people do that in different ways; when singing, dancing, being at peace, being out in nature, knitting, making love, even watching football! We all have our own source of absolute joy that helps us to feel connected to something magical, special and greater than ourselves.

I believe that it helps us every day to find that moment of pure happiness and oneness with the world, but it does not need to take a long time or lots of planning. I do feel we all need to have moments of doing whatever we choose to as though it were the only thing in the world, feeling connected and alive and that nothing else matters.

Self-development questions
1. What are the activities that bring you to that place of connecting with total joy/peace/Divinity?
2. How do you feel when you do those activities? How can you build more of those activities into your everyday life?

Maintaining healthy boundaries

This is always a very difficult yet very important balance to strike as a Spiritual Teacher.

In many professions that involve working with a client and a therapist, or a student and a teacher, it is advocated – indeed expected – that personal relationships will not be formed so as to maintain a clear working professional boundary. In fact, often there is a code of conduct requiring this, which if contravened could have serious implications for a practitioner or teacher. Personal relationships – including friendships – are sometimes allowed in certain circumstances; usually if a significant period of time has passed since the client and therapist were working therapeutically, or the student and teacher were in a learning capacity together.

The purpose of such codes of conduct is to protect both the therapist and the client, or teacher and student, who may be vulnerable.

As Spiritual Teachers, we recognise that some of those who come to our workshops are indeed vulnerable, and so it is necessary to be conscious of your role as a teacher in relation to others, and to maintain healthy boundaries with all.

However, there are also situations where students and teachers become good friends within this sphere of spiritual teaching. Some of the acceptance of the development of friendships is based on the spiritual principle that there is no need for barriers where there is unconditional love for all. Also, the teaching is in an adult context, which has fewer ramifications. The development of friendships can be linked to a need for the teacher or student to feel valued and part of a larger circle of people who understand their spiritual journeys; to a sense of longing for acceptance.

There are, however, some students who are particularly vulnerable. Such individuals – especially those who may be new to their spiritual path – may have been feeling lonely and isolated on their journeys, and are so happy to have found other like-minded people, that they are eager to make friends with every spiritual person that they meet. This can occur before they have had a chance to establish whether they feel that they resonate with and connect with those people. It is rare in my experience, but some students can then quickly develop a dependence on those like-minded people because they are so in need of support. This can include developing a dependence on the teacher, or a perceived need to be regularly in contact with or supported by the teacher.

It is for this reason that I would suggest that any friendships that do develop occur consciously when you have had time to fairly evaluate for yourself whether the friendship is one that is based on equality, or one based on need.

It might perhaps help – initially – to not socialise in the pub after class (and if you do, to not drink alcohol early on in the process of forming relationships). This can allow friendships that do develop to develop naturally over time.

Even with friendships that do develop, it may be advisable to allow the friendship to progress slowly. So for example, if you use Facebook or other social networking sites for close friends only, it may be helpful to preserve that space for close friends until you are ready to welcome newer friends more easily. A quick and easy test of that would be to check with yourself how you would feel if all people could read your status update –

would you mind them seeing it, or not? Of course, if you use social networking for a wider circle of people, this will not matter quite so much.

This becomes increasingly important to manage, the more teaching that you do – because you meet more and more people, many of whom would like to be friends with you, which is a wonderful gift and blessing. You need to ask yourself, however, if you can practically and emotionally be friends with everyone you meet!

Part of developing healthy boundaries involves being clear about your public and your private space. When are you available or 'on duty', and when are you 'off duty'? Some students can feel that we teachers are available all of the time. Often we do work more unsociable hours such as evenings and weekends, but that does not mean that we have to be available all of the time. It can help to publicise when you are available, maybe on your website or in other marketing materials.

If someone calls you outside of these hours and you answer the phone, even if they are in need (unless it is an emergency), it is perfectly acceptable to respectfully ask that they call you at another time that is more convenient for you both. In fact, doing so will help you to maintain your boundaries for yourself and your private life, but also will ensure you have communicated with your student about what they can expect about the support that you can give.

Finally, professional boundaries extend to us being able to consciously know what it is appropriate for us to share in any given situation, as has already been discussed. This is where we need to be aware of how 'our stuff' can get in the way – for example, a lack of self-love, a lack of love for others, unfulfilled emotions or critical judgements, to name a few. These can lead us to be in need of friendships that may not be based on equality.

A final note on boundaries

Boundaries are particularly important to consider from the perspective of co-dependency.

Co-dependence is a relatively new term that has only been used since the mid-1980s. The following information is based on the work of Pia Mellody in her book *Facing Codependence*.

Co-dependency is recognisable by the following characteristics:

1. Difficulty experiencing appropriate levels of self-esteem

2. Difficulty setting functional boundaries (which can include blaming others for our experience, and controlling behaviour)

3. Difficulty owning our reality (seeing ourselves as we really are, or knowing what our thoughts or feelings are)

4. Difficulty acknowledging and meeting our own needs and wants, and being interdependent with others

- It is common to find it hard to say 'no' to others; Pia suggests that a helpful rule of thumb is to help only if you do not support the person's dysfunctional behaviour in doing so, or provoke resentment in yourself.
- We are often out of balance in giving more than we allow ourselves to receive. So, for example, in a workshop, if someone has an emotional reaction and cries, half the room may want to grab a box of tissues, give the person a hug, do something to 'make the person feel better'. We can find it difficult to allow the person to feel and be in their own experience.

5. Difficulty experiencing and expressing our reality moder-

ately (situations and people are either fantastic or dreadful, good or bad).

Co-dependency is a very helpful concept to us as Spiritual Teachers for the following reasons:

a) Many people who come to spiritual workshops may be co-dependent, and so it can further help us to create an environment that maintains healthy boundaries and meets our own needs. Many people are searching for answers – to the problems in their lives, to their childhood abuse, to why they can't maintain loving relationships, why they never felt like they ever 'belonged' anywhere – and can become attached very quickly to you or others, giving their power away.

b) It can support our understanding of the importance of maintaining our own healthy boundaries.

c) We can more easily be aware of our own impact on others, when teaching, if we are aware of any thoughts, beliefs or behaviours that might be co-dependent.

Confidentiality

Every student has the right to expect that their need for confidentiality will be respected – particularly given the sensitive nature of revelations that can occur. In mental health matters, it is expected that the only time that confidentiality will be broken is when someone is at risk of causing harm to themselves or others.

You may wish to share stories or anecdotes as examples of your experiences for your students; however, do not reveal the names of people or any other feature that could lead to them being identified without their consent.

The importance of continuing self-development

If you find yourself in a situation where you feel the need for help and support from others – because of an over-familiar student, for example – ensure that you have a close network of peers that you can ask for advice from. You can ask for advice without revealing names of students or other identifying characteristics. It can be an illustration of our strength, wisdom and consciousness to acknowledge our limitations!

It is also important that we maintain our experience as students, and continue to learn and grow. I feel that it helps us to push ourselves a little out of our own comfort zone – just as our students do – once in a while; learning about something that wouldn't usually resonate with us!

If we are not prepared to try new things, and continue to learn and grow ourselves, then can we ask our students to do the same with us?

Spiritual hygiene

As teachers, we are responsible for facilitating a space that is safe for all to learn and develop, to experience healing and growth. This includes ensuring that the space is safe energetically as well as physically. A safe energetic space is one that is clear energetically of lower-frequency (or 'denser/heavier') energies. If a lot of lower-frequency energies are being released as part of emotional releases or healing (e.g. anger), you can very easily enable those energies to be transmuted – changed – into higher-frequency energies, so that other students, and the space itself, are not affected by the release work.

For more information on this, please refer to the chapters on Grounding and Protection, and Energetically Cleansing the Teaching Environment.

Respecting and honouring students for where they are on their journey

All of us are at different stages of our growth and development in all areas of our lives. I have sometimes come across teaching where students have been invalidated by the teacher for not knowing something, or not being considered to be 'healed' or 'grounded' or 'Light' enough. This can make students feel very small about themselves, and can lead to a loss of confidence and motivation. It helps to honour those who seek to learn and grow and develop, valuing all aspects of what they have learnt so far.

Sometimes that means that you might need to discuss some subject areas that may seem very basic to you; however, this can help ensure that your students have a broad knowledge base and are able to then confidently engage with all of the opportunities to experience new learning that you make available.

I would suggest that it is not for us to judge where our students are on their journeys; that it is for us to honour and respect them for wherever they find themselves to be. None of us is 'perfect', or 'healed', or 'only Light' – we are all trying to do our best with what we have; from our experiences and perspectives.

Also we can get so used to helping and guiding others that it can make it difficult for us to stand back and let someone experience challenges. Part of respecting others involves knowing when to allow someone to learn through challenge, rather than making the journey easier for them; intervening can sometimes prevent a student fully learning in a way that is empowering for them.

Dealing with Challenging Situations

In this chapter, we will consider some of the situations – in particular, behaviours – that we can encounter as Spiritual Teachers, and how we can motivate students to make full use of the learning opportunities available to them.

Before we do so, I will consider the reasons why people may behave in ways that may be challenging for us as teachers to manage.

As Spiritual Teachers, we all encounter situations where we think 'Erm ...what do I do *now*?!' It can be easy to respond to these with human frustration, because a student is Not Behaving Themselves In The Way WE Want Them To. However, the students who are most challenging are – I believe – some of our greatest gifts, for we can really learn a lot about others, ourselves and our own capabilities. They really are our teachers; students who challenge us in some way help us to grow.

Students who challenge us usually don't consciously want to make the learning experience more difficult for themselves, others, or you. They may be facing challenges in some other aspect of their lives, and they are bringing this into the learning environment.

They may feel anxious, fearful, confused, frustrated, uncertain, indecisive, tired or scared for many reasons that are likely to have nothing to do with your course; however, the learning opportunity that you provide may provide a vehicle for students to explore some of their less favourite feelings and experiences, and so they may be vulnerable to behaving in challenging ways.

The question here is more about how you can remain in a place of empathy, acceptance, compassion, understanding and your Truth – and responsibility to each individual – when challenging situations arise.

In his book *Dealing with Difficult Participants*, Bob Pike describes how there are two aims when dealing with challenging behaviours:

1. If possible, to get the participant on board, and

2. To minimise any 'negative' impact that the individual might have on others.

Pike goes on to describe the importance of prevention. This includes:

a) Ensuring that students clearly understand what to expect from the session – creating a positive, safe learning environment. This includes plenty of pre-course information, and being clear about principles that are designed to maintain a safe, respectful environment

b) Setting up the room in a way that encourages equal participation. Being aware of group dynamics; most of us crave acceptance, acknowledgement and the support of our peers

c) Focusing on how the learning can be applied by the students to their lives – in other words, making sure it is relevant.

d) This chapter now considers a range of behaviours or attitudes that can challenge us and other students, and suggests ways that the individuals can be motivated to behave in less challenging ways.

The expert
Those with a sense of expertise can feel as though they are

experts for different reasons:

- they might be newly spiritually awakened and believe that they know everything and must share it with everyone for everyone else's benefit
- they may want to dominate the group, and take centre stage
- they may be connecting strongly with their ego selves
- they may feel that they have 'special' knowledge, insights or connections that they perceive others don't have

The behaviour of 'the expert' can include the following:

- being preachy / proselytising
- finding it difficult to appreciate that others may have already learned similar or different lessons
- assuming that they know everything that there is to know
- constantly sharing their experiences
- finding it difficult to accept others' viewpoints or experiences
- being very enthusiastic about their message
- challenging your teaching
- rejecting (and possibly judgemental) of others and where they are on their journeys. In some cases in the spiritual arena, this can extend to judging much of everyday human existence (e.g. 'work', the news and TV in general, swearing, others who are not consciously on their spiritual journey, and so on).

Ways to motivate:

- This is a situation where prevention is always better than cure! Ensure that you set clear principles and expectations at the start of each session. In my experience, this is the single most important and beneficial thing you can do to ensure that a respectful environment is created.

- Reinforce behaviours that are respectful of the students and the learning environment.
- Allow the individual to share what they would like to share and then move on.
- Remind the individual (and the group) that everyone will have their own individual experiences, which may be different from those of others; that all experiences are valid.
- Facilitate small-group work where possible, to reduce their impact on others – and you may wish to rotate any group leaders if there are small-group exercises.
- Make full use of pauses – as soon as the individual pauses, say 'Thank you for that', and/or 'Let's hear what others have to say about this too', and clearly break eye contact with them as a way of communicating that this is a point for them to sit back and listen. Direct your eye contact to others.
- Thank the individual for their contributions, and then invite others to share their experiences. You can use your language to direct attention away from the individual; e.g. 'What does everyone/anyone else think?'
- Ask the student to share the source of their learning.
- Walk towards and closely to the individual – the closer you physically get, the more quickly someone stops talking. If you remain seated, sit forward and upright to energetically be more in your own strength.
- Physically position yourself so that you are standing between the individual and the other students if possible – this can be easily achieved if you are walking around your environment. This can reduce the flow of energy between this individual and the rest of the class, reducing the power that they are seeking to obtain.

- If the behaviour continues, you can choose to have a quiet word in private, asking the individual to be mindful of the need for everyone to have an equal opportunity to share and learn.

Students who feel blocked intuitively

One of the most common situations experienced by those seeking to connect with their intuition is that they try so very hard, that they make it more difficult for themselves to connect with it. Students who are consciously blocked can experience the following:

- Finding it difficult to experience Divine connections or communication
- Being frustrated with themselves and putting themselves down
- Being disappointed with themselves, you as a teacher, or the course
- Having strong self-beliefs about not being able to see/feel/hear
- Comparing themselves to others

It usually doesn't help them that, in my experience, there is often a student in the same group who has no expectations because they are newer to developing their intuition, and they are having amazing experiences!

Ways to motivate:

- Clearly explain to students how intuition can be received – often students don't recognise how much they *do* experience on a regular basis. For example, Divine communication that they receive using their gut feelings, or from signs, posters, other people, TV or dreams

- Ask all students to just 'give it a go'. It doesn't matter what happens – this is just a safe space to try new things
- Invite students to let go of the expectations that they are placing on themselves
- Invite students to not question the information that they receive – remind them that it does not matter if it makes sense or not, just to allow it through, and the more that they allow through without questioning, the more information that they are likely to receive
- Take a positive attitude to the abilities of others yourself, and communicate your belief that they can do it
- Praise individuals for what they achieve – and keep your focus on positive achievements
- Ensure that students are fully grounded
- Share your own experiences of how you have found it challenging sometimes, and what helped you to remove blocks
- Invite other students to share what helps them to open themselves intuitively

The sceptic

This type of student may:

- challenge you on every detail
- complain a lot
- be excellent at bringing problems to your attention
- take the attitude that 'this doesn't work!'
- help to make sessions more lively and stimulating for everyone, including yourself

Ways to motivate:

- Recognise the importance of using discernment and checking what resonates – and that some things may not resonate, which is perfect; in this way, having a sceptical student can be very helpful to you and everyone else

- Diffuse any questioning by saying 'This may not work for you, but I will share with you how it has worked for me and for others'
- Remain in a place of humility – if you start to become defensive or react from a place of your ego being hurt, you can invite more questioning and scepticism from this individual and others in the group; this can change the energy and dynamics of the whole session, and affect the learning of everyone involved
- Allow the individual to voice their opinions and then to move on
- Give practical examples, or references to more scientific evidence
- Ask the student to allow themselves to experience the course, and then to decide if it resonates with them at the end
- Have a private discussion afterwards or during a break.

The quiet student
This student:

- does not contribute easily
- avoids eye contact
- may be introverted or withdrawn
- may write continuously
- seems physically and energetically reserved and maintains a distance from other participants

Ways to motivate:

- Smile and give eye contact
- Thank them for any contributions that they do make, but

without overemphasising

- Privately check their experiences and learning and ask if they have any questions

There may not be an issue with anything – the student just may be a reflector.

Students who give their power to you

It can be very flattering when a student thinks that you are an amazing teacher, or?guide! They can, however, in the process give their power over to you. As was discussed in the chapter on Ethics, it is important to ensure that you maintain boundaries and develop any friendships slowly over time.

This student may:

- be very enthusiastic about your teachings
- want to become your friend very quickly
- feel the need to ask for your advice on a regular basis, on all aspects of their life
- wish to be more like you than be like themselves
- be seeking answers and be vulnerable
- not feel confident in themselves – sometimes there may be a low self-esteem, which can be covered up with strong social behaviours
- be co-dependent
- try to energetically absorb some of your energies – usually this is unconscious

Ways to motivate:

- Remain loving and supportive, and encourage the student to remember that they are their own best teacher and guide
- Ensure that you share your attention with everyone else –

you can do this with your body language, including breaking eye contact

- Avoid socialising with the group until the boundaries are clear
- Encourage the individual to connect with their own answers rather than the ones that you might suggest – this is important in seeking to prevent the development of any dependency on you, and helps to empower the individual
- Be clear as to when and how you are available to your students – and when you are not available
- Maintain your own energetic cleansing and protection

You may find that some of these students seem to be ungrounded – please refer to the chapter on Grounding and Protection regarding this.

Students with clear mental health problems

Most of us will experience a mental health problem at some point in our lives. Indeed, sometimes it is as a result of having a mental health problem that we experience a spiritual awakening.

This is a very sensitive area, particularly in more esoteric forms of spiritual teaching, which can include channelling or connecting with beings of Light. This is because currently most mental health professionals would consider these activities to be similar to experiencing a delusional or pathological event. This is, I feel, a question of different belief systems challenging each other rather than anything to do with mental health *per se*. In most cases, and in my experience, well-grounded people can have strong esoteric experiences that are not a sign of having a mental health problem. Many students may have some degree of mental health problem, but are conscious about remaining grounded on their journey.

There are, however, some individuals who do have a clear mental health problem that prevents them from being able to ground into the present. My experience of this is rare; however, it does happen. It is not within the remit of this book, or indeed any of us, to diagnose this. If you do have a student who is particularly ungrounded, or who is finding it hard to connect with being in the present, or who appears to have grandiose claims about their own abilities relative to others, then reiterate the principles that you have established, and follow the guidance that is listed under the section on 'The expert'. You may also wish to explore questions around being grounded with the individual, supporting them to identify ways in which they can connect with the present moment more effectively.

If you feel that the individual may be better off spending time on grounding in their own lives before attending your sessions, it is also an option for you as a teacher to suggest this. Indeed sometimes this may be the best option. This can be controversial, as often there is an expectation that we should open our learning opportunities to all, and not exclude anyone. However, sometimes, it may be of more help to some individuals, and the others in their workshop, to ensure that they are more balanced before opening themselves up to more powerful energetic experiences.

For teachers of opportunities where channelling, astral travelling, and/or connecting with other beings can occur, it is important that we approach our sessions with a sense of responsibility to our students, to ensure that they are energetically safe throughout the experience. Please refer to the session on Grounding and Protection for this.

Self-development questions

1. What behaviours would prevent you from being in a place of unconditional love, compassion and acceptance as a Spiritual Teacher?
2. What conditions do you place on your students as a teacher?
3. Do all of these conditions reflect the attitudes that you aim to have with your students? If not, why not, and what can you do about them?
4. How can you come back to a place of unconditional love and compassion as a teacher as quickly as possible when challenged?

Organising Retreats and Residentials

When organising residentials, it helps to get someone that you know to help you – this will be particularly helpful with larger events.

The more that you are able to communicate about what students can expect, the more easily they will be able to settle into the environment and with the group as quickly and easily as possible. Here are some helpful types of information that you could give your students (preferably in advance):

- Clear and easy-to-follow instructions on how to get to the venue. It is likely that someone will forget the instructions, and/or get lost or be delayed – so do expect your phone to ring as people arrive! You can gently remind people to make sure that they bring the map and directions with them before they come
- Information about the sleeping arrangements – who, how many, where and so on
- Information about access to washing facilities. If there are several people sharing a shower, for example, it can help to communicate this so that students have an awareness that they are sharing facilities with others.
- Information about food – what and when!
- A clear understanding of which parts of the venue space can be used by students, and which parts are private (e.g. for other residents only)
- The presence of animals at a venue – for example, a student might have a fear of dogs, or an allergy to cats, so it is important that individuals do know about any animals or pets
- What to expect from extra-curricular activities, if there are any

- If you are using an outdoor space, any additional clothes/equipment that might be helpful (e.g. wellies!)
- If you are at a venue that is seeking to be environmentally friendly, you may wish to invite people to only bring environmentally friendly toiletries – or provide these yourself
- Retreats can be very intensive. Students can expect to have a lovely opportunity for 'time away', perhaps even perceiving the experience as a potential holiday. However, usually due to the intensive nature of healing or development work that takes place and because they are away from home in a different bed, students can find that they don't sleep well. Also there is no easy 'escape' home and away from others at the end of the day, so this can also bring issues up more intensely. This can lead to students who expected a restful holiday to be disappointed, so it can help to let students know about this beforehand, so that their expectations aren't as high. I have been told of a retreat where little sleep is actively encouraged – only four hours on the night before day one – so that people's issues are brought to the surface more quickly because they are tired, and they can then be addressed!
- Do remind people that they are in a shared space with other people, and invite them to be considerate of the needs of others as a result.

Facilitating the development of others is such an honour and privilege, but can also be exhausting because you need to be focused and conscious of the needs of a number of people simultaneously. For this reason, you might find it really helpful to ensure that you create your own personal space and/or time away from students to meet your own need for rest.

Producing Information Accessibly

The following suggestions about presenting information can help your students to read, absorb and process written information that you produce as quickly and easily as possible. This can be information that you present in the form of handouts, workbooks, emails, PowerPoint presentations, on flipcharts and on your website.

The suggestions are based on the 'See It Right' guidelines available through the Royal National Institute for Blind People (RNIB) and guidelines produced by the Employer's Forum on Disability. Many other factors can be involved than are listed here; please bear in mind that these are very simplified guidelines. There is, in fact, a whole branch of graphic design that focuses on the style and design of every aspect of a font, and how that impacts on how our brains process each letter, word and message. We will not be going into that level of detail here; these suggestions are simply designed to bring accessibility in written communication to your awareness, and ensure that your students find it as easy and quick as possible to get information from what you produce.

1. Align text to the left – including headings

Do align all text to the left. For example:

What is love?
Emotions and experiences related to a sense of strong affection – pleasure, passion, commitment, caring, desire, and intimacy.

Avoid centralising information. For example:

What is love?
Emotions and experiences related to a sense of strong affection

– pleasure, passion, commitment, caring, desire, and intimacy. *Why:* Most people in English-speaking countries read from the left of the page to the right. When all of the text is aligned to the left, the eyes and brain know exactly where to go to at the start of every line. When text is centralised, the eyes and the brain have to search for the start of each line, 'jumping' to a different start point from line to line – this can be uncomfortable and confusing for readers with visual impairments, dyslexia, and anyone who finds reading more difficult.

2. Use unjustified text

Do use unjustified text (by clicking the format button 'align left' in most word-processing programs) – this causes the right side of the paragraph to appear 'rugged' and uneven, but the spaces between each word are exactly the same size. For example:

What is love?
Emotions and experiences related to a sense of strong affection – pleasure, passion, commitment, caring, desire, and intimacy
Oxford English Dictionary definition:
'an intense feeling of deep affection or fondness for a person or thing; great liking'
Different definitions in different cultures, e.g. in Greek, there are different words, corresponding to four main types of love:
Erotic, platonic, familial or romantic

Avoid centralising information (using the 'justified' format button) – this causes the right side of the paragraph to look 'neat' and even, by arranging the words so that the spaces between words are different sizes. For example:

What is love?
Emotions and experiences related to a sense of strong affection – pleasure, passion, commitment, caring, desire, and intimacy

Oxford English Dictionary definition: 'an intense feeling of deep affection or fondness for a person or thing; great liking'
Different definitions in different cultures, e.g. in Greek, there are different words, corresponding to four main types of love: erotic, platonic, familial or romantic

Why: When using unjustified (left aligned) text, the spaces between the words are all the same sizes. The eyes and brain know how far to move to get to the next word. When reading justified text, the eyes and brain have to move to a distance that is different from the last time – this can be uncomfortable and confusing for readers with visual impairments, dyslexia, and anyone who finds reading more difficult.

3. Avoid underlining whenever possible

For example:

What is love?
Emotions and experiences related to a sense of strong affection – pleasure, passion, commitment, caring, desire, and intimacy
Oxford English Dictionary definition: 'an intense feeling of deep affection or fondness for a person or thing; great liking'

Why: The added line makes it more difficult to focus on and read letters and words. The eyes and the brain see 'a word with a line under it' rather than 'a word'. They therefore have to work harder to separate the word from the line to read it. This can again be uncomfortable and confusing for readers with visual impairments, dyslexia, and anyone who finds reading more difficult.

4. Avoid using italics whenever possible

For example:

What is love?
Emotions and experiences related to a sense of strong affection –
pleasure, passion, commitment, caring, desire, and intimacy
Oxford English Dictionary definition: 'an intense feeling of deep
affection or fondness for a person or thing; great liking'

Why: The slant of each line and letter changes the 'weight' of the
font, making it lighter and less 'solid'. Again, the eyes and brain
therefore need to work harder to identify the letters and words.
This can again be uncomfortable and confusing for readers with
visual impairments, dyslexia, and anyone who finds reading
more difficult.

5. Avoid using capital letters to emphasise whole words

For example:

WHAT IS LOVE?
EMOTIONS AND EXPERIENCES RELATED TO A SENSE
OF STRONG AFFECTION – PLEASURE, PASSION,
COMMITMENT, CARING, DESIRE, AND INTIMACY.
OXFORD ENGLISH DEFINITION: 'AN INTENSE FEELING
OF DEEP AFFECTION OR FONDNESS FOR A PERSON OR
THING; GREAT LIKING'

Why: In English-speaking countries, we are taught to read words
that use small case letters, only using capitals at the start of
sentences or statements. It takes more effort for the brain and the
eyes to identify words made entirely of capital letters. This can
again be uncomfortable and confusing for readers with visual

impairments, dyslexia, and anyone who finds reading more difficult. If you would like to highlight words, use bold, or increase the size of the font.

6. Avoid shading or pictures behind the body of the text. *Avoid* using shading for large amounts of text.

For example:

> What is love?
> Emotions and experiences related to a sense of strong affection – pleasure, passion, commitment, caring, desire, and intimacy
> Oxford English Dictionary definition: 'an intense feeling of deep affection or fondness for a person or thing; great liking'

Why: Shading or pictures behind the text can reduce the colour contrast between the text and the background. Again, the eyes and brain therefore need to work harder to identify the letters and words from the background. This can again be uncomfortable for readers with visual impairments, dyslexia, and anyone who finds reading more difficult. Highlight words by placing them into a text box or using a larger font size instead.

It is possible to use shading in some circumstances, where the colour contrast remains strong between the background and the text.

7. Use easily readable fonts in an accessible size. *Do use* 'sans serif' fonts, unless you are printing a book.

Why: A serif is a little decorative line that is found on letters in some fonts like Times New Roman. 'Sans serif' means 'without the decorative line on each letter'. Some people find it difficult to read fonts that use serifs, because they distract the eyes and the brain from the overall shape of the letter. The exception here is in the production of books; our brains have become accustomed to reading Times New Roman (a serif font), and it is useable in that context.

Times New Roman is also a very old 'traditional' font, which can communicate 'old and traditional' to the reader.

Font size 12 is considered to be the minimum size at which people read comfortably.

NB: If you are producing documents in large print (for example, font size 14 or 18), avoid using a photocopier for enlargement, as this can send a poor message about the quality of documents that are made available in large print.

8. Use diagrams where appropriate. *Do* use clear diagrams as a useful alternative to words.

Why: A clear diagram can often convey a lot of information, and helps people to understand the message more quickly. Diagrams are useful in this way for all people, and in particular for people with learning disabilities.

Self-development exercise

Practise looking at different information that you read, e.g. leaflets, posters, websites. You can learn to tell if the information is accessible by noticing how comfortably you can read it.

If you feel that your eyes and brain have to work any harder than normal to read or understand the information, the chances are that it is less accessible.

Spiritual Teaching and Legislation

I am not a lawyer or legal adviser but have developed a bit of an interest in legal processes, having been a non-legal adviser with a focus on the Disability Discrimination Act for the Employers' Forum on Disability. The following guidelines have been written to raise your awareness of some of the legal considerations that you may need to make. I would recommend that you seek your own independent legal advice where appropriate.

1. The Equality Act 2010

This new Act came into force on 1 October 2010. It brings together over 116 separate pieces of legislation into one single Act that provides a legal framework to protect the rights of individuals and advance equality of opportunity for all.

The nine main pieces of legislation that have merged are:

- the Equal Pay Act 1970
- the Sex Discrimination Act 1975
- the Race Relations Act 1976
- the Disability Discrimination Act 1995
- the Employment Equality (Religion or Belief) Regulations 2003
- the Employment Equality (Sexual Orientation) Regulations 2003
- the Employment Equality (Age) Regulations 2006
- the Equality Act 2006, Part 2
- the Equality Act (Sexual Orientation) Regulations 2007

The Equality Act has included changes that were not present in the previous Acts that it supercedes. For example, people are now protected from discrimination by association and perception and allowing Positive Action in recruitment and promotion which gives greater scope to address deficits in the workforce.

It uses the term "protected characteristics" to summarise any of the reasons by which discrimination could occur; in other words age, disability, gender reassignment, pregnancy and maternity (including breastfeeding), race, religion or belief, sex and sexual orientation.

"Direct discrimination" is treating someone worse than another because of their protected characteristic. For example, not offering someone a place on a course because they are Sikh.

"Indirect discrimination" can occur if you have a "criterion, provision or practice" that applies to everyone, but causes a disadvantage to people who share a protected characteristic. A "criterion, provision or practice" means anything that you do as part of providing a service to others, from any informal arrangements through to formal policies. Indirect discrimination can be justified if you can show that you acted in a fair and reasonable way in managing your business.

Indirect discrimination applies to all the protected characteristics except pregnancy and maternity.

The following example of indirect discrimination can be found in the Code of Practice (a document produced by the Equality & Human Rights Commission that explains what the law says in ways that ordinary people can more easily understand):

Example: A practising Jew wishes to join a yoga class on a Wednesday evening but the advertising leaflet states that all new members must first take part in a full day's long introductory session which is only available on a Saturday. He is therefore deterred from joining the class because he has to observe the Sabbath. This will be indirect discrimination unless the policy can be justified. (COP Para 5.9).

Discrimination by association

This is a new addition to equality legislation. An example of how discrimination by association could occur is found in the guidance produced by the Equality and Human Rights Commission: A restaurant refuses to serve a customer who has a disabled child with them, but serves other parents who have their children with them.

Discrimination by perception

This is another new addition to equality legislation. You must not treat a person worse because you incorrectly think they have a protected characteristic (perception).

Example: A member of staff in a pub tells a woman that they will not serve her because they think she is a transsexual person. It is likely the woman has been unlawfully discriminated against because of gender reassignment, even though she is not a transsexual person.

Treating people more favourably

The following guidance has been produced by the Equality and Human Rights Commission.

"The Equality Act does allow disabled people to be treated more favourably than non-disabled people in order to help overcome barriers that disabled people face. For example, a local cinema could give two tickets for the price of one to a disabled person who needs an assistant with them.

There are limited and specific situations in which you can provide (or refuse to provide) all or some of your services to people based on a protected characteristic. For example, a butcher who provides halal or kosher meat only for religious reasons is able to continue doing so.

You can also target your advertising or marketing at a group with particular protected characteristics, as long as you do not suggest you will not serve people with a particular characteristic (unless one of the exceptions applies).

You are allowed to provide separate services for men and women where providing a combined service (in other words one where men and women had exactly the same service) would not be as effective. You are also allowed to provide separate services for men and women in different ways or to a different level where:

- providing a combined service would not be as effective, and

- it would not be reasonably practicable to provide the service except in the different ways or to the different level.

In each case, you need to be able to objectively justify what you are doing.

You are allowed to provide single-sex services (services just for men or just for women) where this is objectively justified and:

- only men or only women require the service, or

- there is joint provision for both sexes but that is not enough on its own, or

- if the service were provided for men and women jointly, it would not be as effective and it is not reasonably practicable to provide separate services for each sex, or

- the services are provided in a hospital or other place where users need special attention (or in parts of such an establishment), or

- they may be used by more than one person and a woman might object to the presence of a man (or vice versa), or

- they may involve physical contact between a user and someone else and that other person may reasonably object if the user is of the opposite sex. For example:

- at a commercial gym and swimming pool, women-only swimming sessions could be provided as well as mixed sessions

- separate services for men and women could be provided by a beauty therapist where intimate personal health or hygiene is involved
- a healthcare provider can offer services only to men or only to women, such as particular types of health screening for conditions that only affect men or only affect women.

A business which is providing separate services or single-sex services must not exclude a transsexual person from the services appropriate to the sex in which the transsexual person presents (as opposed to the physical sex they were born with) unless it can objectively justify this, taking into account the needs and wishes of everyone involved. Different treatment in this situation will rarely be justified. You and your staff should take care to avoid a decision based on ignorance or prejudice, as this may lead to unlawful discrimination."

If someone makes a complaint under the Equality Act 2010, it is also unlawful to treat them badly because they have made the complaint. If this ever were to happen, contact your insurers and get legal advice.

Also, if you employ others, or bring in contractors to deliver services to members of the public, you are ultimately legally responsible if they discriminate against a person on any of these grounds. For this reason, it is important to ensure that everyone that you employ is aware of how to treat people fairly. It does not matter if you knew about their actions or do not approve of them. For this reason it is always advisable to have an equality policy and to communicate what behaviours are expected. This can even be included in the contract of employment.

However, you will not be held legally responsible if you can show that:

- you took all reasonable steps to stop an employee acting unlawfully.
- an agent acted outside the scope of your authority (in other words, that they did something so different from what you asked them to do that they could no longer be thought of as acting on your behalf).

The Equality Act and Disability

The term "disability" as defined by the Equality Act 2010 refers to any impairment (physical, sensory or mental) with a substantial and long-term adverse effect on a person's ability to carry out normal day-to-day activities. These can include hearing impairments, visual impairments, mental health problems, diabetes, epilepsy, dyslexia. In some disabled people, memory, the ability to concentrate, learn or understand can be affected.

Reasonable adjustments

The Equalities Act 2010 places a duty on service providers to make reasonable adjustments for disabled people. "Reasonable adjustments" are changes to policies, citeria and practices that place disabled people at a disadvantage, that are reasonable for the service provider to make. Who is responsible for making the adjustments varies according to who provides the workshop and where it is provided.

Adjustments may be needed before, during or after a course to enable a disabled person to make full use of the learning opportunity.

Examples of reasonable adjustments include providing auxiliary aids such as alternative formats or sign language interpreters when this would facilitate the use of the service by a disabled person who would otherwise find it impossible or unreasonably difficult to use the service. Another example is choosing an accessible venue.

For more information, please visit www.equalityhumanrights.com

2. Data Protection Act

For anyone who is practising as a therapist, healer, psychic, medium or in any way with individuals, there is a legal duty to protect the personal sensitive data of any client seeking to use services. This means that the personal information of a client cannot be shared with a third party without their expressed permission. It is always good practice to obtain this permission in writing if ever needed.

Clients also have a right to see any information that is stored about them – including notes of individual healing or therapy sessions, which must be stored safely in a locked place and kept for seven years.

3. The Consumer Protection from Unfair Trading Regulations 2008 (SI 1277)

All who use the services of psychics, mediums and spiritual advisers came under the protection of the new Consumer Protection Regulations which came into force in May 2008.

These regulations were developed to simplify the nature of consumer laws, and repealed many regulations and laws – including most of the Trade Descriptions Act (1968) – as well as the Fraudulent Mediums Act (1951).

The Fraudulent Mediums Act had made it an offence for a person to claim to act as a spiritualistic medium with intent to deceive, or using a fraudulent device.

It was following this that many psychics and mediums began to use disclaimers that stated their services were 'for entertainment purposes only', following a lot of fear-based information around the legal changes. The actual regulations themselves, however, seem to take quite an enabling approach for consumers, and do not seem to be as much of a challenge to mediums and psychics who seek to empower their clients as was initially feared.

The new Consumer Protection Regulations prohibit:

- unfair commercial practices
- the promotion of unfair commercial practices
- 'misleading actions'
- 'misleading omissions'
- aggressive commercial practices

A commercial practice is considered to be unfair if:

a) it contravenes the requirements of professional diligence; and

b) it materially distorts or is likely to materially distort the economic behaviour of the average consumer with regard to the product.
In others words, the Regulations prohibit practices that would:
- cause an individual to change their economic behaviour in ways that they otherwise would not have done
- cause an individual to make a life choice, or change a decision-making process, in ways that they would otherwise not have done, as a result of the trader's practices
- contain false information, or is presented in a way that can cause deception

c) it involves the exploitation by the trader of any specific misfortune or circumstance of such gravity as to impair the consumer's judgment, of which the trader is aware, to influence the consumer's decision with regard to the product.
http://www.opsi.gov.uk/si/si2008/uksi_20081277_en_1

The Committee of Advertising Services (CAP) provides advice under the British Code of Advertising. It advises the following for mediums, psychics and spiritual advisers who wish to market their services:

'Marketers should seek legal advice or contact their Trading Standards Authority to ensure that their claims comply with the law ... [the] regulations make it the marketers' responsibility to prove that they did not mislead or coerce the average consumer and thereby cause them to purchase a product or service they would not have taken otherwise.'

Testimonials do not count as proof that what has worked for one person will work for another. Testimonials can still be used, but only if they are not used in this way.

The CAP advice continues:

5.1 Marketers of services that involve the prediction of the future, or the promise to make specific dreams come true, should advertise their services in a way that is neither misleading nor likely to exploit vulnerable people. Claims that marketers will successfully solve all problems, break curses, banish evil spirits, improve the health, wealth, love life, happiness or other circumstances of readers should be avoided because they are likely to be impossible to prove.

5.1.2 Claims of 'help offered' should be replaced with 'advice' and the emphasis should be on the individual helping him or herself rather than events or changes happening to them as a result of some external force;

5.1.3 Psychics, mediums and religious organisations may be able to make some claims about healing only if it is clear that they are referring to spiritual, not physical, healing;

5.1.4 Marketers should not state or imply that they have personal information or knowledge about recipients of direct marketing e.g. 'I see a major change or a move for you and possibly someone close to you'. They should not imply that they send personalised readings to recipients if the same, or a substantially similar report is sent to everyone who requests a reading;

5.1.5 Marketers should not make claims relating to the accuracy of their readings or claim that results are 'guaranteed' unless they are able to provide evidence to prove the claims;

5.1.6 Claims that a marketer is a personal adviser to royalty, the police, celebrities or wealthy business people or that he or she has been featured on television, radio or in newspapers or magazines should be backed up by adequate and relevant evidence;

5.1.7 Claims that a marketer has been 'established in the UK since ...', '...nobody has been established longer ...', or similar should be backed up by evidence;

5.1.8 Marketers should ensure that the terms of any money-back guarantee are clear and that the guarantee is genuine; and

5.1.9 Testimonials used in marketing communications should be genuine. Testimonials and newspaper articles alone are not sufficient to substantiate claims.

Lucky charms – you cannot claim that an object can do something in particular. You can say 'some people believe ...'

For more information, please visit: www.cap.org.uk

4. Insurance

As a Spiritual Teacher, you need to check with your own insurance company that your insurance covers you for running workshops and courses. Some insurance companies will allow some teaching within standard Professional Indemnity Insurance for practitioners – but may set limits. If you teach more than the limits set, then you may need to get additional cover.

Professional Indemnity Insurance is legally required to practise as a therapist or healer. It protects you in case you are found to be negligent in your dealings with your clients or students, through giving inaccurate advice, information or guidance.

Public Liability Insurance is an additional insurance that you can choose to obtain that covers you in the event of damage to people or property.

Employers' Liability Insurance is needed if you have any employees, whether they be on a part-time, casual or permanent basis.

5. Health and Safety at Work Act (1974)

This Act makes provisions for securing the health, safety and welfare of persons at work, for protecting others against risks to health or safety in the workplace. Depending on individual circumstances, any injury or health and safety risk that a student encounters may result in legal proceedings – but it would be likely to be a personal injury claim rather than a claim under this piece of legislation.

For this reason, it is important that you remain aware and vigilant at all times of the health and safety of all students, including ensuring that:

- fire exits are always clear, and that you know where the fire extinguishers and alarms are
- you know how and where to evacuate students to – should the need arise – and always communicate this to students
- any loose cabling/bags/shoes/obstructions are removed to a place of safety
- any candles that are burning are in a place of safety on a heat-resistant surface.

6. Children's Act 1989 and 2004

All childcare legislation in the UK defines children as those being aged between 0 and 18. Even if a 16 year old is living independently, they are still covered by the Children's Act 1989 and 2004.

If you are running courses specially for children, then you must have a policy on Child Protection, and an Enhanced CRB Disclosure (Criminal Records Bureau). You must have parent's written permission for the child to attend.

If your course is aimed at adults only, then it is advisable that you do not accept anyone under the age of 18, unless they are accompanied by a parent or legal guardian, who gives their written consent for the child to attend.

One of the ways of checking the age of your students is to ask on the booking form. A helpful (and inoffensive) way of asking is to put "Age if under 18".

Remaining Conscious of Our Own Learning Needs: the Importance of Self-Development

Self-development is a crucial part of our own growth and development – and I would suggest it is very closely related to our ability to remain fully present, conscious and responsible teachers of others.

We can establish possible avenues for our own self-development in several ways:

- asking our students to evaluate the content and delivery of our workshops
- evaluating our own course design and performance
- being conscious of what we do not know – which can be triggered by students asking a question that we do not know the answer to
- identifying repeating patterns of behaviour and/or challenges in our own lives, and seeking to continue to heal or work with our own issues

In order to do this, we must be open to receiving feedback from ourselves and others. This requires a careful balance of maintaining our own self-esteem whilst applying humility.

If you don't have a healthy level of self-esteem, you may find that, when evaluating your performance, you only remember the one or two times in a day when you said something that made you cringe, rather than the rest of the day which was a huge success.

The converse of this is not recognising any of your own development needs at all. We all have our 'blind spots': the issues we have that we do not see in ourselves, but that other people can see. A useful model for gauging the size of your own blind spot is the Johari Window.

The Johari Window

The Johari Window model is a simple and useful tool for illustrating and improving self-awareness, and mutual understanding between individuals within a group; it can also be used to assess and improve a group's relationship with other groups. The model was developed by American psychologists Joseph Luft and Harry Ingham in the 1950s, while researching group dynamics. Luft and Ingham called their model 'Johari' after combining their first names, Joe and Harry. Today the Johari Window model is especially relevant due to our emphasis on, and the influence of, 'soft' skills, behaviour, empathy, cooperation, inter-group development and interpersonal development.

The Johari Window is a square divided into four quadrants (or areas), each representing what we and others can identify about ourselves, our feelings, motivations and so on. The Window looks like this:

The four areas show the following information:

1 open/free area	blind area 2
3 hidden area	unknown area 4

1. Open/free area: this is what is known by the person about him/herself and is also known by others (i.e. you can see this information about yourself and other people can see it too)

We are said to be at our most effective as communicators, and in seeking to ensure cooperation, shared learning and growth, when we are in the open area. It is the area where misunderstandings, confusion and conflict are least likely to occur.

2. Blind spot/area: what is unknown by the person about him/herself but which others know (i.e. other people can see this information about you, but you can't see it yourself)

One of the ways of facilitating a conscious awareness of ourselves as Spiritual Teachers is to aim to reduce the size of our own blind spot area. This we can do by becoming more conscious of our own experiences, and seeking feedback from others. This is a very sensitive area for some people, who may have a large blind spot area, and may not be open or ready to receive feedback. Being honest with ourselves can also be a painful process, and therefore one that can tend to be avoided.

3. Hidden area/'façade': what the person knows about him/herself that others do not know (i.e. you know this information about yourself, but you do not share it with others)

This is an area of considerable importance to us as Spiritual Teachers. As we discussed in earlier chapters, there are times when it is appropriate to hold back some of ourselves, to ensure that we have space to heal and work on our own journeys without being so open that we are emotionally needy in front of our students. We do also need to be mindful of maintaining boundaries – it is natural and at times necessary to keep very personal information to ourselves – but this area can also include our sensitivities, fears, hidden agendas, manipulative intentions or secrets. Some hidden information, however, is not very personal, and so can be moved to the open area through the process of 'disclosure'. It is crucial for our own feelings of safety that we decide what we disclose about ourselves, rather than have someone disclose something for us that we are not ready to be publicly known. This is an important consideration in maintaining confidentiality and discretion as teachers, and also in considering students' feelings when giving feedback.

4. Unknown area: what is unknown by the person about him/herself and is also unknown by others (i.e. you don't know this information about yourself and nor do others)

This is the area where there may be feelings, behaviours, attitudes and capabilities. This area can be larger in those who have not had a lot of experience in a certain aspect – which is particularly relevant to us a teachers. Often students come without consciously being aware of their own capabilities, and to begin with, we may not be clear either about what they can do. This area can remain large without encouragement and support from us as teachers, to enable individuals to recognise their abilities, skills and gifts.

The Johari Window Questionnaire and self-development questions
Find out the relative size of each of the four areas with your personal Johari Window by completing the questionnaire in the Appendix.

Once you have had an opportunity to identify the relative size of each area, you can consider the following questions. You may find it helpful to return to this exercise on a regular basis.
1. In what ways are you open as a Spiritual Teacher?
2. How could you be more open in a way that you and your students would be comfortable with?
3. What feedback have others given you that you have

---

previously chosen to ignore, that may help you to understand yourself better and reduce your blind spot area?

4. What do you keep hidden that it would be appropriate for you to share with others?
5. What abilities, attitudes, skills and gifts do you have – both as an individual and as a Spiritual Teacher?
6. What abilities, attitudes, skills and gifts do you have that you find it difficult to acknowledge? Why do you find it difficult to acknowledge these?
7. What abilities, attitudes, skills and gifts would you like to develop further? How can you go about doing so?

The process of evaluation

Evaluation is a hugely important part of self-development as teachers. As well as evaluating ourselves following every session that we facilitate, we can also invite our students to evaluate a session, workshop or course.

The purpose of evaluation is to help identify:

- How well the session/course went in terms of content
- How well the session/course went in terms of delivery
- That the session/course was enjoyable as well as educational
- How well you met the expectations of students
- The quality of materials and resources
- The comfort and suitability of the course environment
- What you can do to improve the session/course next time

It also helps students to feel as if they have some ownership over the course and their part in it – it helps them to feel that it was 'their' course.

The most common ways to evaluate courses are to ask students for verbal feedback, and/or to use 'evaluation forms' or 'happy sheets' (so called because they are designed to establish how happy students are!).

Students are more likely to be open if the feedback can be given anonymously, which is a huge benefit of using evaluation forms as well as asking for verbal feedback. When evaluation forms are handed out, there are often grumbles from students in my experience (because they are usually tired!), but the students do still value knowing that you want their input and feedback. Evaluation forms can also be used as useful tools for inviting students to reflect upon what they have learned. This becomes an additional opportunity for a review, which – as was discussed in the chapter on Accelerated Learning – helps to remind students of their learning, helping to embed it into their long-term memories more easily.

As well as asking students to evaluate the course, you can also do the same as part of your own self-development as a teacher.

Teacher tools

You will find the following in the Appendix:

1. Two examples of evaluation forms that you can give to students
2. A self-evaluation form that you can use after each course that you deliver

---

Appendix

VAK Self-Assessment Questionnaire

Based on the work of Fernald, Keller, Orton, Gillingham, Stillman and Montessori; psychologists who have been developing these models since the 1920s.

Circle or tick the answer that most represents how you generally behave.

(It's best to complete the questionnaire before reading the accompanying explanation.)

1. When I operate new equipment I generally:
a) read the instructions first
b) listen to an explanation from someone who has used it before
c) go ahead and have a go; I can figure it out as I use it

2. When I need directions for travelling I usually:
a) look at a map
b) ask for spoken directions
c) follow my nose and maybe use a compass

3. When I cook a new dish, I like to:
a) follow a written recipe
b) call a friend for an explanation
c) follow my instincts, testing as I cook

4. If I am teaching someone something new, I tend to:
a) write instructions down for them
b) give them a verbal explanation
c) demonstrate first and then let them have a go

5. I tend to say:
a) watch how I do it
b) listen to me explain
c) you have a go

6. During my free time I most enjoy:
a) going to museums and galleries
b) listening to music and talking to my friends
c) playing sport or doing DIY

7. When I go shopping for clothes, I tend to:
a) imagine what they would look like on
b) discuss them with the shop staff
c) try them on and test them out

8. When I am choosing a holiday I usually:
a) read lots of brochures
b) listen to recommendations from friends
c) imagine what it would be like to be there

9. If I was buying a new car, I would:
a) read reviews in newspapers and magazines
b) discuss what I need with my friends
c) test-drive lots of different types

10. When I am learning a new skill, I am most comfortable:
a) watching what the teacher is doing
b) talking through with the teacher exactly what I'm supposed to do
c) giving it a try myself and working it out as I go

11. If I am choosing food off a menu, I tend to:
a) imagine what the food will look like
b) talk through the options in my head or with my partner

c) imagine what the food will taste like

12. When I listen to a band, I can't help:
a) watching the band members and other people in the audience
b) listening to the lyrics and the beats
c) moving in time with the music

13. When I concentrate, I most often:
a) focus on the words or the pictures in front of me
b) discuss the problem and the possible solutions in my head
c) move around a lot, fiddle with pens and pencils and touch things

14. I choose household furnishings because I like:
a) their colours and how they look
b) the descriptions the salespeople give me
c) their textures and what it feels like to touch them

15. My first memory is of:
a) looking at something
b) being spoken to
c) doing something

16. When I am anxious, I:
a) visualise the worst-case scenarios
b) talk over in my head what worries me most
c) can't sit still, fiddle and move around constantly

17. I feel especially connected to other people because of:
a) how they look
b) what they say to me
c) how they make me feel

18. When I have to revise for an exam, I generally:
a) write lots of revision notes and diagrams
b) talk over my notes, alone or with other people
c) imagine making the movement or creating the formula

19. If I am explaining to someone I tend to:
a) show them what I mean
b) explain to them in different ways until they understand
c) encourage them to try, and talk them through my idea as they do it

20. I really love:
a) watching films, photography, looking at art, or people-watching
b) listening to music, the radio or talking to friends
c) taking part in sporting activities, eating fine foods and wines or dancing

21. Most of my free time is spent:
a) watching television
b) talking to friends
c) doing physical activity or making things

22. When I first contact a new person, I usually:
a) arrange a face-to-face meeting
b) talk to them on the telephone
c) try to get together whilst doing something else, such as an activity or a meal

23. I first notice how people:
a) look and dress
b) sound and speak
c) stand and move

24. If I am angry, I tend to:
a) keep replaying in my mind what it is that has upset me
b) raise my voice and tell people how I feel
c) stamp about, slam doors and physically demonstrate my anger

25. I find it easiest to remember:
a) faces
b) names
c) things I have done

26. I think that you can tell if someone is lying if:
a) they avoid looking at you
b) their voice changes
c) they give me funny vibes

27. When I meet an old friend:
a) I say 'It's great to see you!'
b) I say 'It's great to hear from you!'
c) I give them a hug or a handshake

28. I remember things best by:
a) writing notes or keeping printed details
b) saying them aloud or repeating words and key points in my head
c) doing and practising the activity or imagining it being done

29. If I have to complain about faulty goods, I am most comfortable:
a) writing a letter
b) complaining over the phone
c) taking the item back to the store or posting it to head office

30. I tend to say:
a) I see what you mean
b) I hear what you're saying
c) I know how you feel

Now add up how many As, Bs and Cs you selected:

As =
Bs =
C's =

If you chose mostly As you have a VISUAL learning style.
If you chose mostly Bs you have an AUDITORY learning style.
If you chose mostly Cs you have a KINAESTHETIC learning style.

Some people find that their learning style may be a blend of two or three styles; in this case read about the styles that apply to you in the explanation below.

When you have identified your learning style(s), read the learning styles explanations and consider how this might help you to identify learning and development that best meets your preference(s) – this we will do on the course itself.

Learning Styles Questionnaire

This questionnaire, designed by Honey and Mumford (1982), is designed to find out your preferred learning styles. Given that the learning 'habits' that you have picked up during your lifetime so far will affect the way in which you learn, it is important for you to find out your 'habits' so that you can either fit them with a model of learning that suits them, or change them to accommodate other learning styles.

There is no time limit to this questionnaire. The accuracy will depend on how honest you are in answering. Try and answer as *you*, not as *the teacher* or *facilitator* or *leader*.

There are no right or wrong answers. If you agree with a statement more than you disagree, please put a tick by it. If you disagree more than agree, put a cross by it. Be sure to mark each item with a tick or cross.

1. I have strong beliefs about what is right and wrong, good and bad.
2. I often throw caution to the wind
3. I tend to solve problems using a step-by-step approach, avoiding any flights of fancy.
4. I believe that formal procedures and policies cramp people's style
5. I have a reputation for having a no-nonsense, 'call a spade a spade' style
6. I often find that actions based on gut feelings are as sound as those based on careful thought and analysis
7. I like to do the sort of work where I have time to 'leave no stone unturned'
8. I regularly question people about their basic assumptions
9. What matters most is whether something works in practice
10. I actively seek out new experiences

11. When I hear about a new idea or approach I immediately start working out how to apply it in practice
12. I am keen on self-discipline such as watching my diet, taking regular exercise, sticking to a fixed routine
13. I take pride in doing a thorough job
14. I get on best with logical, analytical people and less well with spontaneous, 'irrational' people
15. I take care over the interpretation of data available to me and avoid jumping to conclusions
16. I like to reach a decision carefully after weighing up many alternatives
17. I'm attracted more to novel, unusual ideas than to practical ones
18. I don't like 'loose ends' and prefer to fit things into a coherent pattern
19. I accept and stick to laid-down procedures and policies so long as I regard them as an efficient way to get the job done
20. I like to relate my actions to a general principle
21. In discussions I like to get straight to the point
22. I tend to have a distant, rather formal relationship with people at work
23. I thrive on the challenge of tackling something new and different
24. I enjoy fun-loving, spontaneous people
25. I pay meticulous attention to detail before coming to a conclusion
26. I find it difficult to come up with wild, 'off the top of the head' ideas
27. I don't believe in wasting time by beating around the bush
28. I am careful not to jump to conclusions quickly
29. I prefer to have as many sources of information as possible – the more data to mull over, the better
30. Flippant people who don't take things seriously enough

usually irritate me

31. I listen to other people's point of view before I put my own forward
32. I tend to be open about my feelings
33. In discussions I enjoy watching the manoeuvrings of the other participants
34. I prefer to respond to events on a spontaneous, flexible basis rather than plan things in advance
35. I tend to be attracted to techniques such as network analysis, flow charts, branching programmes, contingency planning etc.
36. It worries me if I have to rush to make a tight deadline
37. I tend to judge people's ideas on their practical merits
38. Quiet thoughtful people tend to make me feel uneasy
39. I often get irritated by people who want to rush into things
40. I think it's more important to think about the present moment than to think about the future or the past
41. I think decisions based on a thorough analysis of all the information are better than those based on intuition
42. I tend to be a perfectionist
43. In discussions I usually pitch in with lots of 'off the top of my head' ideas
44. In meetings I put forward practical, realistic ideas
45. More often than not, rules are there to be broken
46. I prefer to stand back from a situation and consider all of the perspectives
47. I can often see inconsistencies and weaknesses in other people's arguments
48. On balance I talk more than I listen
49. I can often see better, more practical, ways things can be done
50. I think written reports should be short, punchy and to the point

51. I believe that rational, logical argument should win the day
52. I tend to discuss specific things with people rather than engaging in small talk
53. I like people who have both their feet firmly on the ground
54. In discussions I get impatient with red herrings and irrelevancies
55. If I have a report to write I tend to write lots of drafts before I decide on the final version
56. I am keen to try things out and see if they work in practice
57. I am keen to reach answers via a logical approach
58. I enjoy being the one who talks a lot
59. In discussions I often find that I am the realist, keeping people to the point and avoiding 'cloud nine' speculations
60. I like to ponder the many alternatives before making up my mind
61. In discussions with people, I often find I am the most dispassionate and objective
62. In discussions, I am more likely to adopt a low profile than to take the lead and do most of the talking
63. I like to be able to relate current actions to a bigger picture
64. When things go wrong, I'm happy to shrug them off and put them down to experience
65. I tend to reject wild, 'off the top of the head' ideas as impractical
66. It's best to look before you leap
67. On balance I listen more than talk
68. I tend to be tough on people who find it difficult to adopt a logical approach
69. Most times, I believe the end justifies the means
70. I don't mind hurting people's feelings as long as the job gets done
71. I find the formality of having specific objectives and plans

stifling

72. I am usually the life and soul of the party
73. I do whatever is expedient to get the job done
74. I get quickly bored with methodical and detailed work
75. I am keen on exploring the basic assumptions, principles and theories underpinning things and events
76. I'm always interested to find out what others think
77. I like meetings to run along methodical lines, sticking to laid down agenda etc.
78. I steer clear of subjective or ambiguous topics
79. I enjoy the drama and excitement of a crisis situation
80. People often find me insensitive to their feelings

Produced by Peter Honey (1982)

Scoring and interpreting the Learning Styles Questionnaire

The questionnaire is scored by awarding *one point for each ticked item*. There are no points for crossed items. Simply indicate on the lists below which items were ticked

2	7	1	5
4	13	3	9
6	15	8	11
10	16	12	19
17	25	14	21
23	28	18	27
24	29	20	35
32	31	22	37
34	33	26	44
38	36	30	49
40	39	42	50
43	41	47	53
45	46	51	54
48	52	57	56
58	55	61	59
64	60	63	65
71	62	68	69
72	66	75	70
74	67	77	73
79	76	78	80

Totals

| Activist | Reflector | Theorist | Pragmatist |

Interpreting the score

Chart your score from the previous page into the following table, which determines your *preferred* learning style.

Information about those learning styles is contained in the following pages:

Activist	Reflector	Theorist	Pragmatist	
20	20	20	20	
19				
18		19		
17			19	
16	19	18		
15		17	18	Very
14				strong
13	18	16	17	preference
12	17	15	16	
	16			Strong
11	15	14	15	preference
10	14	13	14	
9				
8	13	12	13	Moderate
7	12	11	12	preference
6	11	10	11	
5	10	9	10	Low
4	9	8	9	preference
3	8	7	8	
	7	6	7	
	6	5	6	
2	5	4	5	
	4	3	4	Very low
	3		3	preference
1	2	2	2	

Learning styles

Activists

Activists involve themselves fully and without bias in new experiences. They enjoy the here and now and are happy to be dominated by immediate experiences. They are open-minded, not sceptical, and this tends to make them enthusiastic about anything new. Their philosophy is 'I'll try anything once'. They tend to act first and consider the consequences later. They tackle problems by brainstorming. As soon as the excitement from one activity has died down, they are busy looking for another one. They tend to thrive on the challenge of a new project but become bored by its implementation and longer-term consolidation. They are gregarious people, involving themselves with others, but in doing so, they seek to centre all attention around themselves.

Reflectors

Reflectors like to stand back and ponder experiences and observe them from many different perspectives. They collect data, both first-hand and from others, and prefer to think about it thoroughly before coming to any conclusions. The thoroughness of collection is important and can mean postponing conclusions for as long as possible. Their philosophy is to be cautious. They prefer to take a back seat in meetings and discussions. They tend to adopt a low profile, and often have a distant, tolerant and unruffled air about them. When they act it is as part of a wider picture, taking the past and present and responding to others' views as well as their own.

Theorists

Theorists adapt and integrate observations into complex but logically sound theories. They think problems through in a step-by-step logical way. They assimilate disparate facts into coherent theories. They tend to be perfectionists who won't rest easily until things are tidy and fit into a rational scheme. They tend to analyse and synthesise. They are keen on basic assumptions, principles, theories, models and system thinking. Their philosophy prizes rationally and logic. They tend to be detached, analytical and dedicated to rational objectivity rather than anything subjective or ambiguous. Their approach to problems is consistently logical. They feel uncomfortable with subjective judgements, lateral thinking and anything flippant.

Pragmatists

Pragmatists are keen on trying out new ideas, theories and techniques to see if they work in practice. They positively search out new ideas and take the first opportunity to experiment with applications. They are the sort of people who are brimming with new ideas that they want to try out in practice. They like to get on with things and act quickly and confidently on ideas that attract them. They tend to be impatient with open-ended discussions. They respond to problems and opportunities as a 'challenge'.

How Activists learn

If you have *a preference for the ACTIVIST STYLE* you will learn from activities where:

- There are new experiences/problems/opportunities from which to learn.
- You can engross yourself in short 'here and now' activities such as business games, competitive team-work tasks, role-playing exercises
- There is excitement/drama/crisis and things chop and change with a range of diverse activities to tackle.

- You have a lot of the limelight/high visibility, i.e. you can 'chair' meetings, lead discussions, give presentations.
- You are allowed to generate ideas without constraints of polity or structure or feasibility.
- You are thrown in at the deep end with a task you think is difficult, i.e. when set a challenge with inadequate resources and adverse conditions.
- You are involved with other people, i.e. bouncing ideas off them, solving problems as part of a team.
- It is appropriate to 'have a go'.

As an ACTIVIST you will learn least from, and may react against, activities where:

- Learning involves a passive role i.e., listening to lectures, monologues, explanations, statements of how things should be done, reading, watching.
- You are required to assimilate, analyse and interpret lots of 'messy' data.
- You are required to engage in solitary work, i.e. reading, writing, thinking on your own.
- You are asked to assess beforehand what you will learn, and to appraise afterwards what you have learned.
- You are offered statements you see as 'theoretical', i.e. explanations of cause or background
- You are asked to repeat essentially the same activity over and over again, i.e. when practising.
- You have precise instructions to follow with little room for manoeuvre.
- You are asked to do a thorough job, i.e. attend to detail, tie up loose ends, dot Is and cross Ts.

How Theorists learn
If you have *a preference for the THEORIST STYLE* you will learn

best from activities where:

- What is being offered is part of a system model, concept, theory.
- You have time to methodically explore the associations and interrelationships between ideas, events and situations.
- You have the chance to question and probe the basic methodology, assumptions or logic behind something, e.g. by taking part in a question-and-answer session, by checking a paper for inconsistencies.
- You are intellectually stretched, e.g. by analysing a complex situation, being tested in a tutorial session, by teaching high-calibre people who ask searching questions.
- You are in structured situations with a clear purpose.
- You can analyse and then generalise the reasons for success or failure.
- You are offered interesting ideas and concepts even though they are not immediately relevant.
- You are required to understand and participate in complex situations.

As a THEORIST you will learn least from, and may react against, activities where:

- You are pitchforked into doing something without a context or apparent purpose.
- You have to participate in situations emphasising emotion and feelings.
- You are involved in unstructured activities where ambiguity and uncertainty are high, e.g. with open-ended problems, or sensitivity training.
- You are asked to act or decide without a bias in policy, principle or concept.

- You are faced with a hotchpotch of alternative/contradictory techniques/methods without exploring any in depth.
- You doubt that the subject matter is methodically sound, e.g. where questionnaires haven't been validated, where there aren't any statistics to support an argument.
- You find the subject matter platitudinous, shallow or gimmicky.
- You feel yourself out of tune with other participants, e.g. when with lots of activities or people of lower intellectual calibre.

How Reflectors learn

If you have a preference for the REFLECTOR STYLE you will learn best from activities where:

- You are allowed or encouraged to watch/think/chew over activities
- You are able to stand back from events and listen/observe, e.g. observing a group at work, taking a back seat in a meeting, watching a film.
- You are allowed to think before acting, to assimilate before commenting, e.g. time to prepare, a chance to read in advance a brief giving background data.
- You can carry out some painstaking research, i.e. investigate, assemble information, probe to get to the bottom of things.
- You have the opportunity to review what has happened, what you have learned.
- You are asked to produce carefully considered analyses and reports.
- You are helped to exchange views with other people without danger, e.g. by prior agreement, within a structured learning experience.

- You can reach a decision in your own time without pressure and tight deadlines.

As a REFLECTOR you will learn least from, and may react against, activities where:

- You are 'forced' into the limelight, e.g. to act as leader, chairman, to role-play in front of onlookers.
- You are involved in situations which require action without planning.
- You are pitched into doing something without warning, e.g. to produce an instant reaction, to produce an 'off the top of the head' idea.
- You are given cut-and-dried instructions on how things should be done.
- You are worried by time pressures or rushed from one activity to another.
- In the interests of expediency you have to make shortcuts or do a superficial job.

How Pragmatists learn

If you have *a preference for the PRAGMATIST STYLE* you will learn best from activities where:

- There is an obvious link between the subject matter and a problem or opportunity on the job.
- You are shown techniques for doing things with obvious practical advantages, e.g. how to save time, how to make a good first impression, how to deal with awkward people.
- You have the chance to try out and practise techniques with coaching/feedback from a credible expert, e.g. someone who is successful and can do the techniques themselves.
- You are exposed to a model you can emulate, e.g. a respected boss, a demonstration from someone with a

proven track record, lots of examples/anecdotes, a film showing how it is done.

- You are given immediate opportunities to implement what you have learned.
- There is high face validity in the learning activity, e.g. drawing up action plans with an obvious end product, suggesting shortcuts, giving tips.

As a PRAGMATIST you will learn least from, and may react against, activities where:

- The learning is not related to an immediate need you recognise / you cannot see an immediate relevance / practical benefit.
- Organisers of the learning, or the event itself, seem distant from reality, i.e. 'ivory towered', all theory and general principles, pure 'chalk and talk'.
- There is no practice or clear guidelines on how to do it.
- You feel that people are going round in circles and not getting anywhere fast enough.
- There are political, managerial or personal obstacles to implementation.
- You can't see sufficient reward from the learning activity, e.g. more sales, shorter meetings, higher bonus, promotion.

Divine Communication Style Questionnaire

Source: Doreen Virtue, *Divine Guidance* (1998)

Circle or tick the answer that first enters your mind as the one that most represents how you generally behave.

1. What I first notice about a new acquaintance is:
   a) how the person looks, such as facial expressions, hairstyle, or manner of dress
   b) the sound, tone, and volume of the person's voice
   c) whether or not I feel comfortable in the person's company
   d) whether or not the person has interesting information to discuss with me.

2. The last film I really enjoyed had:
   a) beautiful scenery or attractive actors
   b) great music and expressive voices
   c) a story that moved me emotionally and left me feeling great
   d) a wonderful message that let me learn something new.

3. Which of these phrases are you most likely to say?
   a) 'I see what you mean'
   b) 'I hear what you're saying'
   c) 'This is how I feel about the situation'
   d) 'Let me think about that'.

4. Whenever I am solving a problem, I am most likely to:
   a) visualise different possible solutions
   b) talk to myself, until I come up with a solution
   c) contemplate the situation until I get a feeling of peace
   d) wait for an answer to appear in my mind.

5. My ideal career involves:
   a) artistic endeavours such as painting, drawing, sculpting,

photography, architecture, or filmmaking
b) composing, playing music, or giving speeches
c) counselling, healing, dancing, and/or writing poetry
d) research, science, writing non-fiction books and articles, medicine and/or inventing.

6. What I love most about nature is:
a) beautiful flowers, trees, and other scenery
b) the sounds of birds, animals, the surf, and the wind
c) the scents and the fresh air
d) I don't get out in nature much, but I would like to spend some time alone outdoors.

7. What I'd most like to improve about myself is:
a) my physical appearance
b) my voice
c) how I feel about myself
d) my knowledge about my favourite topic.

8. If I received some extra money, the first thing I would do is:
a) buy something to beautify my life, such as a painting, a piece of jewellery, or new furniture
b) get front-row seats at a performance by my favourite musicians
c) go on a rejuvenating retreat
d) upgrade my computer systems.

9. If I could meet any famous person, living or dead, I'd most want to meet:
a) my favourite movie star
b) my favourite musician
c) an author who made me feel really good about myself
d) a famous inventor who changed the course of history.

10. My pet peeve about restaurants is that they are:
a) too dark, making it difficult to see the menu and my dining companion
b) too noisy, making it difficult to hear the conversation at the table
c) too crowded, making it difficult for me to relax and enjoy myself
d) too expensive, making it difficult for me to understand why I should eat out rather than eat at home.

11. I love to relax by:
a) watching television or a film
b) listening to music
c) soaking in a hot tub
d) reading a good book.

12. When I'm on vacation, I spend a lot of time:
a) taking photographs and/or videos
b) talking to the local residents
c) eating the delicious local cuisine
d) learning about the history of the area.

13. My most important consideration when shopping for a new vehicle is:
a) its appearance: its style, colour and design
b) the sound of the engine, the quality of its stereo system, or the quietness of its interior
c) my comfort and pleasure whilst driving it
d) the rating given to the car by *Which Car* or other consumer researchers.

14. The one essential characteristic of my work environment is that it must:
a) have sufficient lighting

b) be quiet

c) be comfortable

d) have a dedicated telephone line for a computer modem or other access to the internet.

15. The thing I remember most about going to the circus as a child is:

a) the sights of the clowns and the big-top tent

b) the sounds of the calliope music, children laughing, and the circus announcer

c) the smells of popcorn and animals

d) wondering how the tightrope walkers and acrobats could stay so balanced.

Now add up how many As, Bs, Cs and Ds you selected:

As =

Bs =

Cs =

Ds =

If you chose mostly As you have a VISUAL orientation (clairvoyance).

If you chose mostly Bs you have an AUDITORY orientation (clairaudience).

If you chose mostly Cs you have a FEELING orientation (clairsentience).

If you chose mostly Ds you have a COGNITIVE orientation (claircognisance).

Some people find that their orientation may be a blend of two or three types; in this case, you are using more than one means of connecting with Divine communication.

Johari Window Self-Assessment Questionnaire

Please read through the behaviours given below and mark yourself on a scale of 1 to 10 depending on which value you think best reflects your character.

A value of 10 would reflect the behaviour described as being extremely characteristic, 5 as being somewhat characteristic, and 1 as being uncharacteristic.

Score

1. Open and candid in dealings with others
2. Respect and accept others' comments/reactions
3. Tests for agreement rather than assumes it
4. Freely admits when confused or lacking knowledge
5. Keen to reveal own position on issues
6. Takes initiative in asking for others' views
7. Open in describing feelings about others' actions
8. Makes relevant/pertinent contributions to issues
9. Tries hard to understand the feelings of others
10. Encourages feedback on own ideas and actions
11. Openly affectionate in relationships with people
12. Participative and supportive in group work
13. Risks exposing personal information and emotions
14. Welcomes others' attempts to help, even if critical
15. Tries to influence and control activities of others
16. Reluctant to let matters drop, presses for more
17. Displays hostility and anger when annoyed
18. Encourages collaboration in problem solving

19. Spontaneous in speech and expression
20. Helps those in difficulties with expressing themselves

Johari Window summary sheet

Now take the mark you have given in response to each question on behaviour and enter it in the exposure or feedback column as indicated, then plot your arena area on the graph given below.

Exposure	Feedback
1.	2.
3.	4.
5.	6.
7.	8.
9.	10.
11.	12.
13.	14.
15.	16.
17.	18.
19.	20.

Total   **Total**

FEEDBACK

```
         0        25        50        75       100
E    ┌────────────────────────────────────────────┐
X  0 │                                            │
P    │                                            │
O 25 │                                            │
S    │                                            │
U 50 │                                            │
R    │                                            │
E 75 │                                            │
     │                                            │
 100 └────────────────────────────────────────────┘
```

Booking Form Template

Please complete **one** form per delegate.

Delegate details:
Name
Address

Telephone no
Email
Job Title (optional)
Age (if under 18)

Course Booking

Please state below the name(s) and date(s) of the course(s) that you would like to attend.

Name of course:
Date:

Adjustments
Please state if you need any adjustments, e.g. access, dietary,
    BSL interpretation or information in an alternative format

Payment method
In order to confirm the booking, please pay a deposit of 50%
    of the full cost of the course.
You can do so by visiting PayPal and using the email address
    jane@magicteachings.com or pay directly into the
    following account:
    Name: J Magic
    Bank: Happy Bank
    Sort Code: 01 23 45

Account Number: 67891011

Refunds will only be given where cancellations are given in writing (by post or email) at least 14 days before the event (less 25% as a cancellation charge to cover the administration costs).

Payment in full is required before event attendance or during registration on the morning of the event.

Do you require an invoice? Yes / No

You will be sent an email with the joining instructions at least one week before the date of the course.

If you have any other requirements, or questions about the course, please do contact:

J Magic
magic@gmail.com
07910 123456
Many thanks

Evaluation Form Template 1

Thank you for your attendance at this event. In order to ensure that these learning opportunities are as useful and enjoyable as possible, please could you take a few minutes to provide feedback on your experiences. Thank you.

Please rate the following:

	Excellent	Good	Unsatisfactory	Poor
Content of the event	4	3	2	1
Presentation/delivery of the event	4	3	2	1

Resources and handouts provided	4	3	2	1
Comfort of the venue	4	3	2	1
Benefit you gained from it	4	3	2	1
Value for money	4	3	2	1

1. Please list 3 new ideas or skills you have learned as a result of coming on this event

2. In what ways will your life/work be affected/changed as a result of coming?

3. Please use this space to make any suggestions for improvement

4. What would you say to encourage others to do this workshop?

Please turn over ...

How Likely Are You to Attend

How likely are you to attend?   **Very   Probably   Maybe   Not**

A similar workshop with
[this organisation]

this teacher/facilitator

another organisation

Different workshops with
[this teacher/organisation]

another organisation

If you would like to receive more information on other learning opportunities available through [this teacher/organisation], please add your details to this form:

Name
Email address

Please make any other comments you would like to below.

Thank you for taking the time to complete this form.

Evaluation Form Template 2

Please rate the following aspects of the course:

	Poor				Excellent	
Content of the session	1	2	3	4	5	6

Relevance of the course to my current developmental needs	1	2	3	4	5	6
Presentation of the course	1	2	3	4	5	6
Pace of the teaching	1	2	3	4	5	6
The use of materials	1	2	3	4	5	6
Quality of handouts	1	2	3	4	5	6
How well my expectations were met	1	2	3	4	5	6

Please answer the following questions:

1. 3 key ideas or skills that I have developed during the course:
2. I am still unsure about:
3. I would like to find out more about:
4. From this course I would like to make use of:

Please circle the word(s) that describe what you thought of the course:

interesting fun informative boring rewarding useful

insufficient depth inappropriate a waste of time

Please make any additional comments overleaf.

Thank you for taking the time to attend this course and complete this form.

Spiritual Teacher's Self-Evaluation Form

Course title:

Date:

Please rate the following aspects of the course:

	Excellent	Good	Unsatis-factory	Poor
Content of the event	4	3	2	1
Relevance of the course to students' developmental needs (if known)	4	3	2	1
Presentation/delivery of the event	4	3	2	1
Pace of the teaching	4	3	2	1
Resources and handouts provided	4	3	2	1
Comfort of the venue	4	3	2	1
Benefit you gained from it	4	3	2	1

1. The skills that I used well were:

2. The attitudes that I held that empowered the students have been:

3. The experiences and knowledge that I shared that were helpful to the students were:

4. The ways in which I supported and managed the group positively were:

5. The skills that I would like to develop further for next time are:

6. I will do this in the following ways:

7. The attitudes that I would like to develop further for next time are:

8. I will do this in the following ways:

9. The experience and knowledge that I would like to develop further are:

10. I will do this in the following ways:

11. The ways in which I would like to develop how I support and manage the group positively are:

12. I will do this in the following ways:

13. I did well today because:

14. I am an empowering, inspirational teacher because:

Notes

1 I have unfortunately been unable to locate the source of this quote, although I believe it may have been first used by Freud. Answers on the back of a postcard please ... ;)

2 *Merkabah* = a geometric energy field around our body, linking our spirit and body. It is often represented as a star tetrahedron; however, when it is spinning, it looks more like one rounded field of energy.

3 The words 'positive' and 'negative' are used to describe the different cords, which are an illustration of the limitations of language – they are labels that suggest that one is 'good' and the other 'bad'. These labels are judgemental. I use these terms because they are the accepted terms used, but I would suggest working with cords from a place of acceptance rather than judgment whenever possible.

4 Sources: http://pjentoft.com/Universal-20Laws2.html and http://unitedinspirit.groups.vox.com/library/post/6a00f48cf39 926000200fad691e7510004.html

5 Akashic records are records that are said to contain the history of all of the story of the cosmos. We have individual Akashic records that retain information about our soul's journey, including every thought, word or action that we make. There are additional Akashic records for planets, star systems and even Universes. *Akasha* is Sanskrit for 'sky' or 'ether'.

6 Author unknown.

References and Further Reading

Sue Allen (2007) *Spirit Release: A Practical Handbook* O Books

Marcus Chown (2008) *Quantum Theory Cannot Hurt You* Faber and Faber

Irene Dalichow and Mike Booth (1996) *Aura-Soma: Healing Through Color, Plant and Crystal Energy* Hay House

Employers' Forum On Disability (2000) *Producing Accessible Information*

Madonna Gauding (2005) *The Meditation Bible* Godsfield Press

David Hamilton (2005) *It's the Thought That Counts; Why Mind Over Matter Really Works* Hay House

David Hamilton (2008) *How Your Mind Can Heal Your Body* Hay House

Anodea Judith (2004) *Eastern Body, Western Mind* Celestial Arts Publishing

Anodea Judith (1987 and 1999) *Wheels of Life: A User's Guide to the Chakra System* Celestial Arts Publishing

Tom Kenyon and Judi Sion (2006) *The Magdalen Manuscript* Sounds True

National Union of Students (1999) *The National Students' Learning Programme (NSLP): Training for Trainers*

Manchester Nightline (1994) *Training Manual*

Pia Mellody (2003) *Facing Codependence* Harper One

Liz O'Rourke (2001) *Teacher Trainer Tutor; Transforming the Learning Relationship* Management Books 2000

Stewart Pearce (2005) *The Alchemy of Voice* Hodder & Stoughton

Bob Pike and Dave Arch (1997) *Dealing with Difficult Participants* Jossey-Bass/Pfeiffer

Colin Rose (1998) *Accelerated Learning for the 21st Century: The Six-Step Plan to Unlock Your Master-Mind* Dell

Ananga Sivyer (2000) *The Art and Science of Emotional Freedom* Dragon Rising

Doreen Virtue (1998) *Divine Guidance* St Martin's Griffin
Doreen Virtue (2004) *Angel Medicine* Hay House
Christine Westwood (1991) *Aromatherapy – A Guide for home use* Amberwood

Web references

James Harvey Stout – *The Ego*
http://www.theorderoftime.com/politics/cemetery/stout/h/ego.htm

Picture of the atom:
http://www.sciencewithmrmilstid.com/category/physics/matter-properties-of-matter/atomic-structure/

Picture of the aura:
http://www.celestialessentials.co.nz/auramain.html

Communication: Albert Mehrabian
www.kaaj.com/psych
http://www.businessballs.com/mehrabiancommunications.htm
http://en.wikipedia.org/wiki/Communication

Picture of the chakras:
www.reikiclasses.com and www.ehow.com

The Johari Window:
http://www.businessballs.com/johariwindowmodel.htm

The chakras:
http://www.wisdomsdoor.com/hb/hhb-20.shtml
http://www.colorhealing.com/articles/majorchakras.htm
http://www.crystalsareforever.com/chakra/index.php

The aura:
http://www.spiritualplatform.org/sp/misc/theaura.html

http://www.spiritspeaks.co.uk/aura-energy-field.html

'The Human Handbook' James Harvey Stout's work (free comprehensive online tool):
http://www.trans4mind.com/jamesharveystout/

Honey and Mumford's Learning Styles Questionnaire:
http://www.businessballs.com/kolblearningstyles.htm

Kolb's Learning Cycle:
http://www.businessballs.com/kolblearningstyles.htm

BOOKS

6th Books, investigates the paranormal, supernatural,
explainable or unexplainable. Titles cover everything included
within parapsychology: how to, lifestyles, beliefs, myths,
theories and memoir.